DELIVERANCE MINISTRY

International Catholic Charismatic Renewal Services
Doctrinal Commission

Mary Healy

Deliverance Ministry
by the Doctrinal Commission of ICCRS

ICCRS
Palazzo San Calisto
00120 Vatican City
tel.: +39 06 6988-7126/27
fax: +39 06 6988-7230
e-mail: info@iccrs.org
web site: www.iccrs.org

**Published in the United States by the National Service Committee
of the Catholic Charismatic Renewal in the U.S. Inc.**

To order more copies of this book please contact:

**Catholic Charismatic Renewal
National Service Committee**
Chariscenter USA
PO Box 628
Locust Grove, VA 22508
800-338-2445
Email: chariscenter@nsc-chariscenter.org

Cover design:
Stacy Innerst, Pittsburgh, Pennsylvania, USA

Contents

Preface

Deliverance ministry is one of the gifts of the Holy Spirit that testify to the abundance of grace granted by God to the whole Church through Catholic Charismatic Renewal.

Wherever the Gospel is proclaimed, there the Kingdom of God spreads its light and peace and emits its immense healing powers. Throughout its many decades of experience, Catholic Charismatic Renewal has experienced that the proclamation of the good news about the love of God the Father, who forgives humankind through Jesus the Son, frees people from their sin, allows them to share in God's nature by filling them with the Holy Spirit, and calls them to new life as children of God. In other words, the encounter with Jesus Christ, who rose again and lives, transforms people's lives. As a consequence, whilst they come to have great awareness of God's mercy and of their dignity as God's children, they also acquire a clearer understanding of the dark points in their lives that are impediments to communion with God, with all men and women, and to a Christian life lived to the full. As the Gospel reminds us, the presence of the light of the Word brings out the darkness that is within us (cf. Jn 1:5).

Many people evangelized by Catholic Charismatic Renewal soon become aware of their inner resistance and of unresolved issues. They come to see that there are spiritual bonds holding them captive and experience the difficulty or even an inability to free themselves from this burden. Charity inspired by the Holy Spirit gave rise to a desire within the Charismatic Renewal, right from the outset, to pray for the release of these men and women from their spiritual bondage and to help them with the inner struggle that was oppressing them. The light that comes from prayer, prudent discernment and experience have shown that in some of these cases the spiritual bondage that plagues people is due to the direct influence of the devil. It is precisely here that the ministry of deliverance belongs. This is a gift of the Holy Spirit present since the time of the early Church.

Deliverance ministry, although it differs sharply from major (or public) exorcism—reserved to a bishop and the priests appointed by him and based on the appropriate ritual—brings about an understanding of the immense healing and liberating power that emanates from the person of Jesus, Son of God, in whose name the deliverance is invoked. It is also a comforting rediscovery of the richness of our Baptism as it makes each of the faithful a member of the body of Christ, a sharer, to some extent, in the divine prerogatives of Christ the Head. Deliverance ministry, in this respect, helps to highlight the important role that the lay faithful can and must play in evangelization, in the maternal mission of the Church to heal the wounds of humanity and in spreading God's Kingdom everywhere and in every social sphere. The mission of the seventy-two disciples who were made partakers in Christ's power to cast out demons (cf. Lk 10:17) prefigures the involvement of all the lay faithful in preaching the Gospel and delivering people from the spiritual interference by Satan that afflicts so many souls.

Some years after the publication of the booklet "Prayer for Healing," I am now pleased to see this new booklet produced by the ICCRS Doctrinal Commission on "Deliverance Ministry." The benefit coming from this booklet moves in two directions, one of which could be expressed as "from the Church to Catholic Charismatic Renewal," in the sense that the Doctrinal Commission maintained a close link with the Church as they prepared the text. The Commission accepted the indications given by the Congregation for the Doctrine of the Faith as well as the advice of many theologians and experts in this field. It took care to base all treatment of the theme on a secure biblical, patristic and magisterial foundation. In this way, the patrimony of doctrine and the pastoral practice of ancient Church tradition serves to enhance the experience of Charismatic Renewal, and deliverance ministry is placed on the sure ground of the faith of the Church. The other direction can be articulated as "from Catholic Charismatic Renewal to the Church." The renewed reflection on deliverance ministry that has been stimulated by long-established practice within Charismatic Renewal can now help the whole Church—laity, clergy and religious—to be more sensitive to this "baptismal gift" given to all of Christ's disciples, that should be appreciated in all its value in the spiritual accompaniment of the faithful.

It is my hope that this booklet will serve as a reliable guide, in particular for those in Catholic Charismatic Renewal who regularly carry out deliverance ministry, serving their brothers and sisters in the faith. I also hope that it can be an instrument for discovering and welcoming this ministry in our times, in the exciting mission of the new evangelization.

Cardinal Kevin Farrell

Prefect of the Dicastery for Laity, Family and Life

Foreword

It is a great joy on behalf of ICCRS to present and recommend this publication not only to Catholic Charismatic Renewal but to the whole Church. It will undoubtedly be a useful resource for all those who are engaged in deliverance ministry and those who wish to reflect more deeply upon the place of deliverance in Jesus' ministry and in the life of the Church today.

This text began as a response to various requests received by ICCRS for information and explanation about deliverance ministry within a Catholic context. In response, our Doctrinal Commission began working on outlining a theological and ecclesial framework and producing some pastoral guidelines for deliverance ministry. These reflections were sent out to various theologians worldwide for further comment and reflection.

In April 2014, ICCRS held a colloquium in Rome on deliverance ministry. This drew together a number of theologians and practitioners from around the globe. It proved to be a time of rich reflection and also provided a platform for exchange and discussion. It was recognized that in this area of ministry, there are a variety of approaches, reflecting the diversity of cultures.

Following the colloquium, the main authors of this text were Dr. Mary Healy, chair of the ICCRS Doctrinal Commission and professor of Scripture at Sacred Heart Major Seminary in Detroit, USA; and Fr. Etienne Vetö, professor of theology at the Pontifical Gregorian University in Rome. The final draft was sent out to the wider Commission before being presented to the Congregation for the Doctrine of the Faith. We were subsequently delighted to receive confirmation from the CDF that our text contains no doctrinal problems.

So it is with great pleasure that I am able to recommend this eagerly awaited document. On behalf of ICCRS, I would like to thank all those who have contributed in any way to this publication. We are especially indebted to Dr. Healy and Fr. Vetö and those who serve so willingly as part of the ICCRS Doctrinal Commission. I also offer a word of gratitude to Cardinal Kevin Farrell, Prefect of the Dicastery for Laity, Family and Life, who in the midst of many demands took the time to read our document and responded so quickly with his inspiring preface.

I am sure that this booklet will prove to be a helpful resource to those in Charismatic Renewal and to all those who seek to understand or practice this important ministry more fully. I am especially delighted that it will be published in the Jubilee year, as we celebrate 50 years of Catholic Charismatic Renewal.

Mrs. Michelle Moran
President of ICCRS
January 2017

1

Introduction

He has delivered us from the dominion of darkness
and transferred us to the kingdom of his beloved Son.

– Colossians 1:13

Pope Francis has surprised many people by speaking frequently on a subject that some had thought was a relic of the past: the devil. In his homilies the Holy Father has repeatedly spoken of the strategies of Satan, how we are to combat them, and how we can obtain victory over the evil one in Christ. He has noted that what is at stake in this struggle is nothing less than the eternal destiny of souls. Jesus came, he said,

> to give us the freedom... from the enslavement the devil has over us... On this point, there are no nuances. There is a battle and a battle where salvation is at play, eternal salvation. We must always be on guard, on guard against deceit, against the seduction of evil.[1]

The Holy Father sees a need to awaken the Church to a spiritual reality that has too often been forgotten. Our life on earth is not only a pilgrimage of faith but also a constant battle against evil and against Satan, the prince of darkness, who continually seeks to draw us away from Christ and make us captive to sin, confusion, bitterness, cynicism, and despair. Yet in Christ we are liberated from the dominion of Satan and empowered to resist his ongoing influence.

Pope Francis' warnings are deeply rooted in Scripture and Tradition. The New Testament has much to say about the works of the devil and how to defeat them in Christ. Catholic tradition offers wisdom and countless examples of spiritual combat, from the exorcisms done by St. Anthony of the Desert, St. Catherine of Siena, and many others, to the principles of spiritual discernment taught by St. Ignatius Loyola. This biblical and traditional teaching provides the essential foundation for discussing deliverance ministry as it is practiced today.[2]

The purpose of this book is to offer both theological reflections on deliverance ministry and pastoral guidelines for carrying it out in accord with Catholic faith. This book is primarily addressed to the Catholic Charismatic Renewal, since most of those who carry out deliverance ministry come from the Renewal.[3] But our hope is that these reflections will prove useful beyond the Renewal and will help broaden an understanding and openness to deliverance ministry throughout the Church.

1.1 Discerning the Signs of the Times

Why is deliverance ministry an urgent topic for the Church in our time? The reflections in this book seek to scrutinize the "signs of the times" in the light of the gospel, as Vatican Council II urged.[4] The remarkable rise of ministries of deliverance in recent years is both a fruit of spiritual renewal in the Church and a response to an urgent need in contemporary society.

The Church in some parts of the world is experiencing a renewal: a new love among Catholics for the Holy Spirit, a mobilization of the laity, a greater thirst to know the Scriptures, a fervor for evangelization, and a growing commitment of time and energy in favor of justice and peace. At the same time, however, there are signs of a growing darkness. In Europe, North America, and Oceania, the widespread abandonment of Christian faith and an increasingly aggressive secularism have created a spiritual vacuum, which many people have sought to fill through occult practices, spiritualism, freemasonry, neo-pagan and New Age spiritualities, or even overt Satanism. A flood of occult and spiritistic materials has poured into bookshops and the internet. Many young people have been exposed to the powers of darkness through Satanic forms of music or video games. In Latin America, similarly, as the practice of the faith has declined there has been an increase in superstition and syncretistic devotions such as Santería and the cult of Santa Muerte. In other areas, especially in parts of Africa and Asia, it is common even among Christians to have recourse to witchcraft, magic, curses, ancestor worship, séances, fetishism, or other occult practices. All these activities can lead people into demonic bondage.

It is not only occult practices, however, that are spiritually dangerous. The spread of a global culture of hedonism and materialism has contributed to a rise in immoral patterns of behavior that can also lead to spiritual bondage, including sexual promiscuity, pornography, excessive consumerism, and drug addiction. These patterns of behavior have in turn contributed to the breakdown of the family, to the point that fewer than half the world's children today live in a home with both of their biological parents. Those who have never experienced a father's love or a stable family life are often deeply wounded and thus more vulnerable to spiritual deception and oppression. In some regions of the world, large groups of people have been traumatized by terrorism, religious persecution, war, ethnic cleansing, or mass migration, leading to further spiritual vulnerability.

At the same time these social changes have been occurring, there has been a marked silence among Catholics regarding demons and their real influence in human life. Theologians and preachers of the last half century have often tended to downplay or outright deny the existence of Satan. This unbelief persists despite the strong affirmations of the Catechism and recent popes.[5] Many priests have been trained in forms of biblical criticism that interpreted the Gospel accounts of demon-possession as simply a primitive way of speaking of mental illness. The result is that many preachers and catechists are uncomfortable speaking about the devil, feeling that such a topic belongs to a more superstitious premodern era.

This silence has created a situation where many Catholics, including priests, lack an understanding of the devil and his strategies. In homilies, catechesis, and faith formation, little is said about how to repel the attacks of the evil one and be freed from his influence. Paradoxically, the silence has also led to an unhealthy fear of the demonic realm, especially among people not well educated in the faith. All these elements of the contemporary situation have led to a vast unmet need for deliverance from various kinds of spiritual bondage and oppression. It is tragic that Catholics in some areas seek out help from spiritualists or shamans for relief from demonic affliction because they do not believe the Church is able to help them—or in some cases, they seek help from the Church and do not find it, since they are in need of neither major exorcism nor professional medical help, but simply deliverance. In some areas Catholics turn instead to Pentecostal and independent charismatic ministries for help.[6] The lack of understanding of deliverance also hinders evangelization when native peoples are more keenly aware of the power of evil spirits than Catholic missionaries are of the liberating power of the name of Jesus. There is an urgent need for the Church to wake up to this grave situation.

While some Catholics have been influenced by such patterns of skepticism and secularization, the biblical, liturgical, and catechetical renewal that led up to the Second Vatican Council has been gaining ground. The Council's fruit is particularly seen in the new evangelization and in the Catholic Charismatic Renewal and other new ecclesial movements. At the heart of this ecclesial renewal is the entry of the laity into their full role and dignity as baptized members of the body of Christ, called to the perfection of holiness and full participation in the mission of the Church.[7]

Deliverance ministry in its contemporary Catholic form arose within the Catholic Charismatic Renewal, a movement that began with an outpouring of the Holy Spirit upon college

13

students in Pittsburgh, Pennsylvania, USA, in 1967.[8] The Renewal is characterized by a life-transforming experience of the presence and power of the Holy Spirit, which is common to lay people, priests and religious. As a "current of grace" (a description reaffirmed by Pope Francis),[9] the Renewal has given rise to a much greater participation of lay people in the mission of the Church, in teaching, in community leadership, and in prayer ministry for others. It has also given rise to an ecumenical impetus, as Catholics have experienced a new level of spiritual fellowship with other Christians, based on a common experience of the Holy Spirit and of deeper conversion to Christ.

It is not accidental that this new awareness of the Holy Spirit also brings a new awareness of unholy spirits and their influence in human life. The Holy Spirit who reveals Christ at the same time gives Christians a deeper sensitivity to all that is opposed to Christ and his kingdom, as well an existential experience of Christ's victory. The Renewal has thus contributed to the rediscovery of an element of Catholic tradition that had long been neglected: that the Christian life involves spiritual combat, and that deliverance from evil spirits is part of the mission that Jesus entrusted to the Church.

Contemporary ministries of deliverance first arose in the context of healing ministry, in response to the needs of those who were troubled by various forms of demonic affliction.[10] In the vast majority of these cases, the demonic influence was less than full possession, and thus major exorcism was neither possible nor necessary. Instead, there was need to help people be released from demonic influence in certain areas of their lives. The founders of these ministries drew on the wisdom of Catholic tradition as well as ideas and practices from other charismatic Christians. Many of these ministries were sound and in full accord with Catholic faith; others, however, were characterized by exaggerations, abuses, sensationalism, or aberrant theological claims. Over the years, as deliverance ministry has matured, many unsound ideas and practices have been abandoned. But there remains a need for guidelines, as well as prudent oversight and discernment on the part of the Church's pastors.

Deliverance ministry is clearly meeting an immense spiritual need in the contemporary world. Through it many people have experienced in a vivid, personal way the truth that Jesus came to set captives free. Just as deliverance was an essential part of evangelization in the early Church, so it is an essential part of the new evangelization today. Despite the various problems and challenges, St. Paul's advice remains ever valid: "Do not quench the Spirit... but test everything; hold fast what is good, abstain from every form of evil" (1 Thess 5:19-22).

1.2   The Scope of this Book

There are a wide variety of models and approaches to deliverance, as may be expected given the diversity of cultural contexts throughout the world and the inexhaustible wealth of gifts distributed by the Holy Spirit. Some people use more confrontational methods of deliverance, some less. Some integrate deliverance more fully with inner healing, some less. The purpose of this book is to offer general principles and guidelines, not to endorse any one model or approach as the only valid one. Moreover, this book is not a how-to manual; it cannot be used as a substitute for training and experience. There are several books available that give more detailed practical instruction on deliverance ministry. The topic of this book is limited to deliverance, not major exorcism.[11] Major exorcism is a liturgical rite of the Church carried out by a bishop or a priest duly appointed by the bishop, for the purpose of liberating the demon-possessed (CCC, 1673; Code of Canon Law, 1172). Deliverance, on the other hand, is carried out by any of the faithful for those experiencing lesser forms of demonic influence.

Finally, this book does not override or replace any guidelines established by a local bishop or national conference of bishops. All Catholics should faithfully follow the directives of their bishops.

1.3   Glossary of Terms

The terminology used for forms of demonic influence and for liberation from them is not completely standardized; some terms are used variously in different regions and by different authors. This book will use the following terms and definitions.

Adjuration: invoking the name of God or Jesus to induce someone to do something. In the context of deliverance, to adjure demons is to command them in the name of God or Jesus to stop afflicting a person or to leave.

Deliverance (also called **simple exorcism**): the effort to free a person of demonic oppression and bondage in the power of Jesus' name. Deliverance is carried out by lay people as well as priests, and does not involve any set form of prayer or liturgical rite of the Church. The term **deliverance ministry** is used (rather than simply deliverance prayer) because this ministry is broader than prayer; it often includes bringing a person into an encounter with Jesus, helping the person bring inner wounds to light and receive Christ's healing, and using direct commands as well as prayers.[12]

Demon (or **evil spirit**): a fallen angel, who was created by God but sinned against God by opposing his reign and now seeks to oppress and destroy human beings.

Demon-possession (or **possession**): an extreme form of demonic bondage in which the demon(s) is able at times to take control over a person's body and to control his or her words and actions. It is important to avoid misunderstanding the term "possession": an evil spirit can never have ownership of a human being, who always belongs to God alone. There always remains some residue of freedom in the person's will.

Deprecative: by means of prayer to God (or the saints), in contrast to imperative.[13]

Devil: the prince of demons, also known as Satan, Beelzebul, or Lucifer.

Exorcism: in a stricter sense, exorcism is synonymous with major exorcism (see below). In a broader sense, exorcism is used to mean any expulsion of demons from a person, whether through major exorcism or simply deliverance.[14]

Imperative: a direct command (in this case, to a demon or demons).

Major exorcism (also called **solemn exorcism** or simply **exorcism**): the expulsion of demons from a person who is demon-possessed through the spiritual authority Jesus entrusted to his Church, performed only by a bishop or by a priest with the permission of the bishop, using the liturgical rite of exorcism.

Minor exorcism: the prayers for liberation from demonic influence that are part of the liturgical rites of the catechumenate and of baptism for children and adults, used either before or during the baptismal ceremony.

Oppression: any form of serious, continuing demonic harassment, which may be physical (for instance, the afflictions of Job) or spiritual (for instance, obsessive thoughts, a deep sense of condemnation, irrational fear, etc., where such thoughts are not due solely to emotional or psychological causes).[15]

Public exorcism: an exorcism performed in the name of the Church with a precise ritual. These include both major exorcisms (performed using the rite of exorcism) and minor exorcisms (performed during the rites of the catechumenate or of baptism).

Private exorcism: a simple casting out of a demon in the name of Jesus, performed neither in the name of the Church nor with a precise ritual; thus synonymous with simple exorcism.

Simple exorcism: *see* deliverance.

Spiritual bondage: an inner demonic influence by which a person's will is bound or constrained to some degree, such that the person is unable to freely choose the good in certain situations. Spiritual bondage involves some degree of consent to demonic influence, whereas oppression does not necessarily involve consent.

2

Biblical Foundations

*But if it is by the finger of God that I cast out demons,
then the kingdom of God has come upon you.*

– Luke 11:20

The New Testament makes clear that Jesus' mission was not simply to forgive sins and call people to a new way of life. In fact, Jesus came to wage war against the ancient enemy of humankind, the devil. His mission was to win the definitive victory over Satan by his cross and resurrection, and to free all those who were under the dominion of darkness because of sin (Col 1:13-14). The First Letter of John sums it up succinctly: "The reason the Son of God appeared was to destroy the works of the devil" (1 Jn 3:8). Christ's work of freeing us *from* sin and Satan is to free us *for* the fulfillment of God's eternal plan: that we would be raised up to share in God's own divine life forever (2 Pet 1:4).

Before he ascended in heaven, Christ commissioned his disciples to extend his victory over Satan to peoples of every time and place. They were to do so through the proclamation of the gospel, leading to faith and baptism, by which people are rescued from Satan's domain and incorporated into the Church (Mk 16:15-16). As Paul describes his commission in

Acts, Christ sent him to the nations "to open their eyes, that they may turn from darkness to light and from the power of Satan to God..." (Acts 26:18).

Deliverance ministry must be understood within this broader context of the biblical teaching on Christ's saving mission and his victory over the dominion of darkness. This chapter briefly summarizes what Scripture reveals about Satan and his works, Christ's victory, and our share in it.

2.1 Satan in the Old Testament

The name Satan is from the Hebrew word *satan*, which means adversary or accuser.[1] It is synonymous with devil, which is from the Greek word *diabolos*, meaning slanderer or accuser.[2] Other biblical names for Satan are Beelzebub, Beelzebul, and Abaddon/Apollyon (2 Kg 1:2; Mk 3:22; Rev 9:11).

Throughout Israel's history there was a growing insight into the mystery of evil. Although Satan is mentioned only rarely in the Old Testament, there was a gradual development of the doctrine of Satan as the archenemy of God and man, who seeks to lead human beings into sin and destruction. In the book of Job, Satan appears as one of the angels in God's heavenly court. He accuses Job of serving God for self-centered reasons, and God permits him to test Job by afflicting him with devastating misfortunes (Job 1). During the reign of David, Satan attempts to destroy Israel by enticing David to take a census, an act of disobedience that has disastrous consequences (1 Chr 21:1-14).[3] On another occasion Satan stands before God to accuse the high priest Joshua, who represents the whole people Israel, but he is rebuked for it by

22

the Lord (Zech 3:1-2). In later biblical tradition, Satan is explicitly identified with the serpent who brought death into the world by tempting Adam and Eve to sin (Wis 2:24; cf. Gen 3:1-6).

There is one apparent case of demonic possession in the Old Testament. An evil spirit torments King Saul, provoking him to maniacal rage and violence so that he attempts to kill David with his spear (1 Sam 18:10-11).[4] Ironically, it is David's playing on the lyre—presumably, playing psalms of praise—that relieves Saul of the demonic torment. On other occasions, evil spirits incite people to treachery, false prophecy, or other evils (Jdg 9:23; 1 Kg 22:22-23).[5] In the book of Tobit the demon Asmodeus, the only demon named in the Bible, kills seven husbands of Sarah; he is finally banished by Tobias using a remedy given by the angel Raphael (Tob 8:2-3).

These passages describe Satan and other demons as real spiritual beings whose aim is to sow evil in the world and thwart God's plans for human beings. But the Old Testament provides no ultimate solution to the problem of evil.

2.2 Jesus' Victory over Satan

The New Testament reveals both the full depth of man's predicament and the magnitude of God's gift of salvation in Jesus Christ.

First, it becomes clear that Satan's evil influence is not merely occasional, extending to a few troubled individuals, but universal. The "whole world"—that is, all human society, which has become alienated from God due to sin—"is in the power of the evil one" (1 Jn 5:19). Satan is "the ruler of this world" (Jn 16:11), "the god of this world" (2 Cor 4:4), and "the deceiver of the whole world" (Rev 12:9). These texts do not mean the world is under the full control of Satan, since God is also at work in the world and he alone has ultimate sovereignty, but rather that every part of earthly reality is in some way touched by Satan. Satan is not a god in the literal sense; he is only a fallen angel, a creature totally subject to God's restraints (cf. 2 Pet 2:4; Rev 12:7-10). But human beings have placed themselves under his dominion through sin (cf. Jn 8:34).[6] Satan exerts his influence through demons, lesser evil spirits who operate under his rule (Mt 9:34), and also through human beings (Jn 13:2) or the structures of human society (Eph 2:2). His kingdom is the kingdom of this world (Lk 4:5-6; Rev 11:15).

At the same time, however, the New Testament announces the glorious good news that Christ has come to inaugurate the kingdom of God and liberate human beings from the dominion of sin and Satan (Col 1:13). By his life, death and resurrection, Christ has broken the power of Satan and ensured his ultimate demise (Jn 12:31; Rev 12:12). "He disarmed the principalities and powers and made a public example of them, triumphing over them in [the cross]" (Col 2:15).

2.3   Exorcisms in the Ministry of Jesus

In the synoptic Gospels (Matthew, Mark and Luke), Jesus' confrontations with demons play a remarkably prominent role in his public life. Indeed, the casting out of demons was one of Jesus' most characteristic activities. In Mark, Jesus' very first act of ministry is an exorcism in the synagogue at Capernaum (Mk 1:21-27).[7] When the Gospels summarize Jesus' ministry in Galilee, they nearly always mention the casting out of demons along with teaching and healing.

That evening, at sundown, they brought to him all who were sick or possessed with demons.... He healed many who were sick with various diseases, and cast out many demons; and he would not permit the demons to speak, because they knew him. (Mk 1:32-34; cf. Mt 8:16)[8]

He went throughout all Galilee, preaching in their synagogues and casting out demons. (Mk 1:39)

Whenever the unclean spirits beheld him, they fell down before him and cried out, "You are the Son of God." And he strictly ordered them not to make him known. (Mk 3:11-12; cf. Lk 4:41)

He came down with them and stood on a level place, with a great crowd of his disciples and a great multitude of people from all Judea and Jerusalem and the seacoast of Tyre and Sidon, who came to hear him and to be healed of their diseases; and those who were troubled with unclean spirits were cured. (Lk 6:17-18)

In that hour he cured many of diseases and plagues and evil spirits, and on many that were blind he bestowed sight. (Lk 7:21)

Jesus' exorcisms are in striking contrast to the exorcisms that were practiced among first-century Jews (cf. Mt 12:27;

Acts 19:13).[9] Whereas Jewish exorcisms typically made use of incantations, holy objects, and prayers, Jesus' exorcisms were by a simple word of command, spoken on his own authority: "He cast out the spirits with a word" (Mt 8:16).

Jesus announces to the onlookers the significance of these mighty works: "If it is by the finger of God that I cast out demons, then the kingdom of God has come upon you" (Lk 11:20). His exorcisms are eschatological signs—signs visibly demonstrate the arrival of the kingdom of God and the downfall of the kingdom of Satan.[10] Jesus is the stronger one who by his cross and resurrection binds the "strong man," Satan, and plunders his house—that is, frees those who were captive to him (Mk 3:27). No one has to live captive to evil any longer.

Jesus' self-description in his inaugural sermon in the synagogue at Nazareth places healing and deliverance at the heart of his messianic mission. He reads a passage from the prophet Isaiah and proclaims its fulfillment in himself: "The Spirit of the Lord is upon me, because he has anointed me to preach good news to the poor. He has sent me to proclaim liberty to the captives and recovering of sight to the blind, to set at liberty those who are oppressed, to proclaim the acceptable year of the Lord" (Lk 4:18-19). In this context the "captives" and "oppressed" refer to all who are in bondage to sin and its effects, including both unjust social structures and various forms of demonic oppression (cf. Isa 58:6; Lk 1:77).[11] Luke thus portrays Jesus' ministry in terms of healing and deliverance. Jesus came to deliver human beings from everything that keeps them from the fullness of life that God intended for them. St. Peter, in a sermon in Acts, likewise puts deliverance at the center of Jesus' mission: "God anointed Jesus of Nazareth with the Holy Spirit and with power. He went about doing good and healing all that were oppressed by the devil, for God was with him" (Acts 10:38). The Gospels give detailed accounts of several individual exorcisms, each of which reveals unique aspects of Jesus' work of salvation.

2.3.1 The Exorcism in the Synagogue

Jesus' first exorcism is of a demonized man in the synagogue at Capernaum (Mk 1:21-24; Lk 4:33-34). Although the Evangelist gives no background information about this man, presumably he is a regular synagogue attendee. He may have seemed an ordinary person, whom others would not have guessed was troubled by demons. But in the presence of Jesus the hidden evil is exposed, precisely so that it can be expelled.

The reaction of the witnesses is significant: "And they were all amazed, so that they questioned among themselves, saying, 'What is this? A new teaching! With authority he commands even the unclean spirits, and they obey him'" (Mk 1:27). Their response shows an awareness of the intrinsic connection between Jesus' teaching and his authority to dispel demons. The truth itself—the revelation of the good news of God and his plan—when proclaimed with authority, has power to liberate people from captivity to evil. This in turn implies that spiritual bondage can be rooted in deception that becomes deeply rooted in people's hearts and minds (cf. Rom 1:21, 25; Eph 4:14, 22).

2.3.2   *The Man Possessed by a Legion*

The most dramatic exorcism in the Gospels is that of the Gerasene demoniac (Mk 5:1-20; cf. Mt 8:28-34; Lk 8:26-39). This episode vividly portrays the destructiveness of demonic bondage. The tormented man's existence among the tombs, crying out and bruising himself, is an image of self-hatred, rage and despair. Human society is powerless to help; even binding him in chains proves ineffective, since the man breaks the chains, displaying the superhuman strength that sometimes occurs in cases of demonic possession (Mk 5:7, 9, 10, 12).

The Gerasene man is an extreme example of bondage to evil, yet on a symbolic level he is an image of all fallen humanity, wounded and disfigured by the consequences of sin.[12] His wretched condition illustrates the fact that Satan's goal is to deface and destroy the image of God in human beings. His deliverance, on the other hand, is an image of what Christ's work of salvation accomplishes for all who believe in him.

The demons' plea not to be sent out of the country suggests that evil spirits are able to attach themselves to certain geographical regions (cf. Mt 12:43-45; Tob 8:3). Although Jesus permits them to enter a herd of swine, this proves to be their undoing when the swine stampede down the bank into the sea and are drowned. Since evil spirits seek "waterless places" (Mt 12:43), their submersion in the depths of the sea is an appropriate fate—one that recalls the great event in biblical history when the oppressors of God's people were drowned in the depths of the sea (Ex 14).

The liberated man epitomizes the result of being freed from demonic bondage by Jesus. He is now "clothed," his degradation and shame taken away and his human dignity restored. He is "in his right mind," able to reason clearly and interact normally with others. Even more, he is commissioned by Jesus to evangelize: "Go... and announce all that the Lord has done for you." Having experienced Jesus' liberating power for himself, he becomes a witness to others, visible to all as healed and full of joy. Indeed, the effectiveness of his testimony appears from the new openness Jesus meets on his second visit to the area (cf. Mk 5:17 and 7:31–8:9). This story illustrates the extraordinary evangelistic power of personal testimonies given by those who have been delivered from demons by Jesus (cf. Mk 16:9-10).

2.3.3 Exorcisms in Answer to a Parent's Plea

Two of the exorcisms recorded in the Gospels are done in response to the pleas of a distraught parent.

The Canaanite woman who begs Jesus to heal her demonized daughter (Mt 15:22-28; cf. Mk 7:25-30) is a gentile, and thus an outsider to the covenant. Although Jesus at first responds with only a rebuff—"It is not fair to take the children's bread and throw it to the dogs"—the woman is relentless on behalf of her daughter. Her response displays both humility and boldness: "Yes, Lord, yet even the dogs eat the crumbs that fall from their masters' table." Far from being annoyed at her audacity, Jesus is delighted. "O woman, great is your faith! Be it done for you as you desire." This episode illustrates the effectiveness of persistent, faith-filled prayer.

It also demonstrates that Jesus does not need to be physically present to exercise his liberating power.

The second case is that of the father who pleads for his epileptic son (Mk 9:14-29; cf. Mt 17:14-20; Lk 9:37-43). The Evangelist's description seems to indicate a combination of demonic oppression and mental or neurological illness. Jesus questions the father, perhaps as a way of discerning the entryway for the demonic affliction: "How long has he had this?" The father's response indicates that it was a lifelong condition. Jesus rebukes the "mute and deaf spirit," which probably indicates that the spirit had rendered the boy himself incapable of speech or hearing. Because the affliction was recurrent, in this case Jesus commands the demon not only to come out but also to never enter him again. As often occurs in Jesus' exorcisms, the spirit departs in bluster and a show of contempt, throwing the boy into convulsions. Yet it is powerless before the Lord's command.

This episode ends with an important lesson for the disciples. They had been unable to cast out the spirit themselves. Afterward they ask Jesus privately, "Why could we not cast it out?" In Mark's version Jesus answers, "This kind can only come out by prayer and fasting" (Mk 9:29).[13] In Matthew's version his response is, "Because of your little faith. For truly, I say to you, if you have faith as a grain of mustard seed, you will say to this mountain, 'Move from here to there,' and it will move; and nothing will be impossible to you" (Mt 17:20). These may seem to be two entirely different answers, but in reality they are not. Jesus implies that this boy was afflicted by a particularly powerful or entrenched demon, against which great faith had to be exercised. Faith is strengthened by prayer, and prayer is in turn empowered by fasting, which helps to strip Christ's disciples of self-reliance, earthly attachments, and all that weakens their spiritual authority in Christ.

2.3.4 Exorcisms in Relation to Healing

In several cases the Gospels attribute a physical condition to a demonic cause. After healing the woman who was bent over, Jesus describes her as "a daughter of Abraham whom Satan bound for eighteen years" (Lk 13:16). The Gospels recount the healing of "a mute demoniac," that is, one whose inability to speak was caused by a demon (Mt 9:32-33; cf. Lk 11:14), and "a blind and dumb demoniac," one whose double disability had a demonic cause (Mt 12:22). As mentioned above, the epileptic boy seems to have suffered from both neurological or mental illness and demonic affliction.

In other cases, there seems to be a suggestion of demonic influence but without a definite attribution. Jesus "rebuked" the fever of Peter's mother-in-law (Lk 4:39), the same verb used for rebuking demons (Lk 4:35, 41), which may mean that an evil spirit had caused or contributed to the fever.[14] The same word "rebuke" is again used for Jesus' stilling of the storm (Lk 8:24), suggesting that demonic powers somehow instigated the storm that threatens to deflect him and his disciples from their mission.

These Gospel passages suggest that caution is warranted regarding the sharp distinction that is sometimes made today between demonic affliction and affliction due to merely natural causes. The Evangelists claim that evil spirits are a contributing factor in some, though by no means all, disabilities and illnesses. There is no basis for the assertion that the biblical authors were unable to distinguish between demonic affliction and physical or mental illness. Jesus healed other mute, deaf and blind people where there is no suggestion of demonic causality (e.g., Mk 7:32-35; 10:46-52). The majority of Jesus' healings take place without any hint of the involvement of evil spirits. The Gospels frequently mention Jesus' exorcisms in distinction from his healings (Mt 4:24; Mk 1:32-34; Lk 4:40-41).

2.4   Exorcism in the Mission of the Disciples

During his public life Jesus chose twelve apostles and commissioned them to share in his saving mission. It is significant that the first task with which he charged them was the casting out of demons: "He called to him his twelve disciples and gave them authority over unclean spirits, to cast them out, and to heal every disease and every infirmity" (Mt 10:1; cf. Mk 6:7; Lk 9:1). This commission indicates that the apostles (and later, their successors the bishops) share in a unique way in Jesus' authority to overcome the evils that afflict human life. Correspondingly, they have a unique responsibility to minister that healing power to the sick, the afflicted, and the demon-possessed.

Jesus sends the apostles out with the charge, "Preach as you go, saying, 'The kingdom of heaven is at hand.' Heal the sick, raise the dead, cleanse lepers, cast out demons" (Mt 10:7-8; cf. Lk 9:2). Just as in his own ministry, the good news of the kingdom is to be proclaimed not only in words but also in deeds of power that demonstrate the truth of the words.

The preaching of the gospel, when received in faith, carries a divine power to *accomplish* that which it announces: salvation from sin and Satan, reconciliation with God, eternal life. Deliverance from demons is therefore an intrinsic part of evangelization.

Mark's version of the sending of the twelve emphasizes the close connection between deliverance from demons and repentance from sin. "They went out and preached that people should repent, and they cast out many demons..." (Mk 6:12-13). Only by turning away from sin in sincere repentance can people experience true spiritual liberation, since it is primarily through sin that demons gain a foothold in human lives. Deliverance without repentance is temporary and ultimately illusory.

Although the ministry of casting out demons is exercised with particular authority by the apostles, it is not limited to them, just as evangelization is not limited to them. Luke records that Jesus later commissioned a larger group of seventy disciples[15]—a foreshadowing of the share of all the lay faithful in Christ's mission. He gave them the same charge: "Whenever you enter a town and they receive you... heal the sick in it and say to them, 'The kingdom of God has come near to you'" (Lk 10:8-9). Luke reports the outcome of their mission:

> The seventy returned with joy, saying, "Lord, even the demons are subject to us in your name!" And he said to them, "I saw Satan fall like lightning from heaven. Behold, I have given you authority to tread upon serpents and scorpions, and over all the power of the enemy; and nothing shall hurt you. Nevertheless do

not rejoice in this, that the spirits are subject to you; but rejoice that your names are written in heaven." (Lk 10:17-20)

Jesus' answer reaffirms the authority of his disciples over the powers of evil, and their protection from demonic retaliation. At the same time it is a warning against the temptation to pride or to an excessive focus on the demonic realm. Their spiritual authority is a gift from him, not something they possess independently. Their joy should not be in their triumphs over the enemy but in their destiny of eternal life with God.

At the end of the Gospel of Mark, the risen Lord Jesus explicitly extends to all believers the authority to heal and cast out demons.

And he said to them, "Go into all the world and preach the gospel to the whole creation.... And these signs will accompany those who believe [i.e., Christians]: in my name they will cast out demons; they will speak in new tongues; they will pick up serpents, and if they drink any deadly thing, it will not hurt them; they will lay their hands on the sick, and they will recover." (Mk 16:15-18)

Now all believers, filled with the Spirit of the risen Lord, are gifted with divine protection and supernatural power for their mission to proclaim the good news in word and deed.

In one Gospel episode, a person who does not belong to the band of disciples is found casting out demons in Jesus' name. John complains to Jesus and says, "we forbade him because he does not follow with us" (Lk 9:49; cf. Mk 9:38). Jesus' reply directs his disciples to take an expansive rather than a restrictive approach toward others who are acting in his name: "Do not forbid him; for he that is not against you is for you" (Lk 9:50). The disciples should not presume to restrict the invocation of Jesus' name, "for no one who does a mighty work in my name will be able soon after to speak evil of me" (Mk 9:39).

2.5 Exorcism in the Apostolic Church

The Acts of the Apostles describes how the early Christians, led by the apostles, faithfully carried out Jesus' commission to evangelize. At the beginning of Acts, the risen Lord gives the apostles his final instructions before ascending into heaven: "You shall receive power when the Holy Spirit has come upon you; and you shall be my witnesses in Jerusalem and in all Judea and Samaria and to the ends of the earth" (Acts 1:8). It is only by the power of the Holy Spirit that they will be able to evangelize with divine efficacy, preaching the gospel accompanied by signs and wonders that convince the hearers of its truth. After the descent of the Spirit at Pentecost, the apostles begin to preach with the same boldness and supernatural power that characterized Jesus' public ministry.

Among the deeds of power performed by the apostles, and later by other Christians, are the casting out of demons. "The people also gathered from the towns around Jerusalem, bringing the sick and those afflicted with unclean spirits, and they were all healed" (Acts 5:16). When the deacon Philip evangelized in Samaria, it was his healings and exorcisms that moved his hearers to believe the gospel. "The multitudes with one accord gave heed to what was said by Philip, when they heard him and saw the signs which he did. For unclean spirits came out of many who were possessed, crying with a loud voice; and many who were paralyzed or lame were healed" (Acts 8:6-7). Likewise when Paul preached the gospel in Ephesus, "God did extraordinary miracles by the hands of Paul, so that handkerchiefs or aprons were carried away from his body to the sick, and diseases left them and the evil spirits came out of them" (Acts 19:11-12).

Acts records one exorcism in detail. As Paul and Silas are evangelizing in Philippi, they encounter "a slave girl who had a spirit of divination[16] and brought her owners much gain by fortune-telling" (Acts 16:16). This description affirms that fortune-telling (like other occult activities) is not an innocent pastime, but a dangerous involvement with evil spirits. In this case, the demonized girl is being exploited by others for financial gain. She follows Paul and his companions, shouting, "These men are servants of the Most High God, who proclaim to you the way of salvation." Her cry is doctrinally correct, but proves a distraction and obstacle to the work of evangelization. Paul does not act immediately but waits several days, perhaps to ensure accurate discernment. Finally, provoked at the hindrance to his mission and the owners' cynical exploitation of a young girl, he "turned and said to the spirit, 'I charge you in the name of Jesus Christ to come out of her.' And it came out that very hour" (Acts 16:18). As demons were compelled to obey Jesus, so they are powerless before the word of command given by a disciple in Jesus' name.

Another episode in Acts clarifies what it means to act in Jesus' name. In Ephesus, Paul's miracles and exorcisms are so impressive that some non-Christians decide to imitate him.

Some of the itinerant Jewish exorcists undertook to
pronounce the name of the Lord Jesus over those who
had evil spirits, saying, "I adjure you by the Jesus
whom Paul preaches." Seven sons of a Jewish high
priest named Sceva were doing this. But the evil spirit
answered them, "Jesus I know, and Paul I know; but
who are you?" And the man in whom the evil spirit
was leaped on them, mastered all of them, and over-
powered them, so that they fled out of that house na-
ked and wounded. (Acts 19:13-16)

This episode raises the question, why do these men suffer
humiliating defeat, whereas the unnamed exorcist in the
Gospel (Lk 9:50) is approved by Jesus? The likely reason is
that the latter acted with authentic faith in Jesus, whereas the
sons of Sceva were using Jesus' name as if it were a magic
formula. To act in Jesus' name is not to use a formula but to
act *under his lordship*, by his delegated authority. The sons of
Sceva evidently had no personal relationship with "the Jesus
whom Paul preaches" and were not acting in obedience to
him. Jesus warns in the Sermon on the Mount, "On that day
many will say to me, 'Lord, Lord, did we not prophesy in your
name, and cast out demons in your name, and do many
mighty works in your name?' And then I will declare to them,
'I never knew you; depart from me, you evildoers'" (Mt 7:22-
23). The sobering truth is that it is possible to perform supernatural deeds in Christ's name and yet be on the path
toward damnation.

2.6 Deliverance and Christian Life

The New Testament proclaims that by his cross and resurrection Christ has decisively triumphed over sin, Satan and death. However, it is obvious that evil continues to exist in the world and that Satan's final demise is yet to come. Christ's work of salvation will be complete only at the end of time, when he "delivers the kingdom to God the Father after destroying every rule and every authority and power" (1 Cor 15:24). Until then, Satan is still permitted to operate in the world. The whole creation groans in travail, awaiting the fullness of redemption (Rom 8:22), while the evil one is continually at work seeking to undermine Christ's kingdom and seduce people toward destruction, knowing his time is short (Rev 12:12).

During this time between Christ's ascension and his return in glory, Christ gives the members of his body the privilege of sharing in his combat and his victory over Satan. The New Testament thus speaks frequently of our struggle against demonic adversaries. The Christian life is a spiritual battle in which we are to fight against the evil one and grow progressively free of his influence in our lives (Eph 6:10-17; 1 Pet 5:8-9; cf. CCC 405). By ourselves we would have no hope of success, yet in Christ we are assured of victory. "For though we live in the world we are not carrying on a worldly war, for the weapons of our warfare are not worldly but have divine power to destroy strongholds" (2 Cor 10:3-4).

2.6.1 Kinds of Demonic Activity

The New Testament discloses the strategies of Satan and the various ways in which he operates in human hearts and in the world. At the same time, Scripture teaches Christians how to prevail against the devil. Part of Christian catechesis is making the faithful aware of the devil's strategies in order "to keep Satan from gaining the advantage over us, for we are not ignorant of his designs" (2 Cor 2:11).

Satan's most obvious activity is **temptations to sin**. Satan tempted Jesus himself after his baptism, seeking to entice him to pursue worldly acclaim instead of the messianic mission given by the Father, which would involve suffering and death (Mt 4:1-11; cf. 16:23). Jesus' refusal of these temptations was the prelude to his ultimate victory on the cross. Likewise Satan continually seeks to tempt both believers and unbelievers toward sins such as pride, greed, and sexual immorality (cf. 1 Tim 3:6; 6:9; 1 Cor 7:5). In particular, the evil one tries to seduce Christians to turn away from the faith (1 Thess 3:5). The First Letter of Peter warns, "Your adversary the devil prowls around like a roaring lion, seeking someone to devour" (1 Pet 5:8).

Satan also acts by means of **deception**, making evil appear desirable and making God appear to be the adversary of our happiness, just as he did with Eve in the garden (cf. 2 Cor 11:3). This is why Jesus calls Satan "a liar and the father of lies" (Jn 8:44). He continually seeks to blind people's minds to the truth (2 Cor 4:4; Rom 1:21) and thus rob them of the freedom and fullness of life that God desires for us. Satan even disguises himself as an angel of light (2 Cor 11:14). Those who follow his deceitful counsel may become liars themselves, as did Ananias and Sapphira (Acts 5:3; cf. 2 Tim 3:13). Paul warns that Satan's deceptions can come in the form of false teachings that lead people astray from the authentic doctrine of the Church. Such teachings may sound appealing but are actually "doctrines of demons" (1 Tim 4:1; cf. Col 2:8; 2 Tim 4:3; Rev 2:24).

Fear is another means by which the evil one keeps people in bondage. The letter to the Hebrews declares that Jesus came to "destroy him who has the power of death, that is, the devil, and deliver all those who through fear of death were subject to lifelong bondage" (Heb 2:14-15). "Fear of death" alludes to fear not only of physical death but of every circumstance that makes us conscious of our mortality—pain, deprivation, weakness, criticism, opposition, failure, loss. These fears influence many human choices on a subconscious level, often leading to escapism, addiction, and other destructive efforts at self-protection.

One of the most prominent ways Satan keeps people in spiritual bondage is through unresolved **anger or unforgiveness** of past offenses. Although the emotion of anger is not in itself sinful, holding on to it is. Paul cautions that if we harbor anger in our heart we give a foothold to the evil one: "Be angry but do not sin; do not let the sun go down on your anger, and give no opportunity to the devil" (Eph 4:26-27).[17] Jesus warned that the servant who refuses to forgive his fellow servant will be "delivered to the jailers" (Mt 18:34), which may allude to spiritual torment in this life as well as after the final judgment.

The evil one is also able to act by means of **external obstacles and attacks**, especially those that hinder the evangelistic mission of the Church. Jesus speaks of Satan as one who sows weeds in God's field, and who snatches away the word of God from some of those who hear it (Mt 13:19, 38-39). Satan prevented Paul from going to Thessalonica (1 Thess 2:18), tormented him with a "thorn in the flesh" (2 Cor 12:7), and obstructed his preaching of the gospel by means of Elymas the magician and the fortune-telling girl (Acts 13:8-10; 16:16-18). In the book of Revelation Jesus tells the church in Smyrna that the devil will throw some of them into prison (Rev 2:10). As mentioned in Section 2.3.4, demonic causes can also sometimes underlie physical or mental illnesses. In extreme cases, the devil can even take control of a person's body, as in the exorcisms recounted in the Gospels.

Finally, the gravest form of demonic influence is seen in those instances where a person has apparently given full **consent of the will to evil**. This occurs particularly in the case of Judas, whom "Satan entered into," inducing him to betray Jesus (Jn 13:27). A similar consent to evil is implied in Peter's rebuke of Ananias: "Ananias, why has Satan filled your heart to lie to the Holy Spirit...?" (Acts 5:3; see also Paul's rebuke of Elymas in Acts 13:10). Whereas the demon-possessed people in the Gospels clearly desire to be set free, in these other cases the person has freely embraced evil and shows no desire to be set free.

2.6.2 Means of Overcoming the Evil One

Jesus warned his disciples that the evil one does not give up occupancy willingly:

> "When the unclean spirit has gone out of a man, he passes through waterless places seeking rest; and finding none he says, 'I will return to my house from which I came.' And when he comes he finds it swept and put in order. Then he goes and brings seven other spirits more evil than himself, and they enter and dwell there; and the last state of that man becomes worse than the first." (Lk 11:24-26)

This warning applies not only to the exorcised but to all those redeemed in Christ. To become a Christian is to be liberated from the grip of Satan in one's heart and life. But far more importantly, it is to be filled with the Holy Spirit and become a living temple of God. The indwelling of the Spirit, which begins at baptism, must be maintained and continually deepened if we are to avoid falling again under Satan's influence (Gal 5:1).

The most important way of gaining progressive freedom from Satan's influence, then, is to be filled with the Holy Spirit and to grow in holiness so that there is no place for the evil one to get a foothold. This occurs through all the avenues of grace given by God, including prayer, the practice of virtue, repentance, participation in the liturgy and sacraments, and the mutual support and encouragement of the body of Christ (cf. Eph 4:26-32; 5:15-16; 6:18; Heb 10:24-25).

Prayer is a powerful weapon against the enemy. In the Our Father, Jesus taught his disciples to pray, "deliver us from evil." The phrase can also be translated "deliver us from the evil one," that is, Satan (CCC 2851). Jesus himself prayed for his disciples on the night before he died: "I do not pray that you take them out of the world, but that you keep them from the evil one" (Jn 17:15). Christians are to pray with great confidence to their heavenly Father, asking for protection from the enemy and all his schemes (cf. 2 Tim 4:18).

Forgiveness—letting go of judgments, resentments, and grudges—is another crucial means of defense. If harboring anger gives a foothold to the devil (Eph 4:27), then conversely, forgiveness removes that foothold. In the Christian community, practicing mutual forgiveness disables the strategies by which Satan seeks to divide and tear down (2 Cor 2:10-11).

Scripture explains how to position ourselves when under spiritual attack: we are to "stand" and "resist" the devil. It is the Lord who fights for us, as Moses told the Israelites when they were trapped by Pharaoh's army at the Red Sea: "Fear not, stand firm, and see the salvation of the LORD, which he will work for you today.... The LORD will fight for you, and you have only to be still" (Ex 14:13-14). So James counsels, "Resist the devil and he will flee from you" (Jas 4:7), and Peter exhorts, "Resist [the devil], firm in your faith..." (1 Pet 5:8).

Paul teaches that to be able to resist, we must clothe ourselves in "the armor of God," that is, all the saving gifts by which God has made us his holy people:

> Put on the whole armor of God, that you may be able to stand against the wiles of the devil. For we are not contending against flesh and blood, but against the principalities, against the powers, against the world rulers of this present darkness, against the spiritual hosts of wickedness in the heavenly places. Therefore take the whole armor of God, that you may be able to resist in the evil day, and having done all, to stand.

Stand therefore, having girded your loins with truth, and having put on the breastplate of righteousness, and having shod your feet with the equipment of the gospel of peace; besides all these, taking the shield of faith, with which you can quench all the flaming darts of the evil one. And take the helmet of salvation, and the sword of the Spirit, which is the word of God. (Eph 6:11-17)

Finally, as described above, Christ has given his followers authority to cast out demons from those in bondage to them: "in my name they will cast out demons" (Mk 16:17). The primary context for the casting out of demons is evangelization, since we are to proclaim the good news of Christ accompanied by mighty deeds by which God bears witness to its truth (Heb 2:4). The casting out of demons demonstrates that Jesus Christ is Lord and that he has triumphed over every opposing power and principality.

It is important to recognize, therefore, that although believers are summoned to defend ourselves against the devil, the Church's fundamental stance is not defensive but offensive. Jesus promised Peter that "the gates of the netherworld shall not prevail" over his Church (Mt 16:18; cf. Gen 22:17). Gates are a last defense against an advancing army. Jesus is declaring that Satan is in retreat. The Church will advance with the good news of salvation to the very doors of the netherworld, which will not be able to stand against it. Christians are to walk in peace, confidence and victory, not in fear and anxiety about what Satan might do next. For "we are more than conquerors through him who loved us. For I am convinced that neither death, nor life, nor angels, nor principalities... will be able to separate us from the love of God in Christ Jesus our Lord" (Rom 8:37-39).

3

Theological Context

*The reason the Son of God appeared was to destroy
the works of the devil.*

– 1 John 3:8

In recent decades there has been a great deal of theological and pastoral reflection on exorcism, but relatively little on deliverance. Yet the remarkable expansion of this ministry in the last half century calls for ongoing reflection in light of Christian faith. How is it that evil spirits are able to influence and oppress human beings? What does their activity have to do with sin? What is deliverance, and how does it relate to God's overall work of salvation? To address these questions requires embracing both of the aims of Vatican Council II: *ressourcement* (a rediscovery of the ancient sources of faith, especially the Scriptures, the liturgy, and the Fathers of the Church) and *aggiornamento* (presenting the Christian faith in the most effective way for the present-day context).

This chapter offers some brief theological reflections on deliverance, without claiming to speak the final word. There is need for continuing study and reflection to discern what God is doing today and to integrate it within the living tradition of the Church.

3.1 Deliverance in a Wider Perspective

Deliverance from evil spirits must be understood in the wider context of Christ's whole saving work made present and operative through the Church. Deliverance is intrinsically linked to salvation from sin. It is a sign of God's saving power that gives great effectiveness to evangelization, and it is a gift of God's mercy leading toward the full freedom and happiness he wishes for all human beings.

3.1.1 Deliverance in God's Work of Salvation

We are created for communion with the triune God through our conformation to Christ, already in this life and fully in everlasting life—and this embraces communion with others as well. Eternal life is an exchange of love: receiving God's love and loving him in return. But we are acutely aware of the obstacles to this design: sin, structures of sin, physical woes and sufferings, inner wounds, and demonic forces. Salvation thus has two dimensions: a "negative" one, which entails being freed from the evils that hinder our communion with God and with others, and a "positive" one, which entails being transformed in Christ and raised up to share in God's own life. The latter is the fullness of God's plan, while the first is a means toward that end. We are freed *from* evil to be free *for* love and eternal life.

Among the kinds of evil from which we need to be liberated, sin is the most serious because it is a refusal of God's love and disobedience to his will, made with the full weight of our free choice and personal responsibility. The core of liberation is thus conversion and the forgiveness of sins. Deliverance from evil spirits is another aspect of the "negative" dimension of salvation, one that is closely linked to deliverance from sin. Sometimes demonic bondage—for instance, an inability to trust God, or a deep-seated insecurity—leads us to sin, or directly hinders us from growing in a loving relationship with God or others. In this case, deliverance is part of the process of being freed from sin and fighting against it. Deliverance is not only about our own well-being but also about our communion with God and others.

Two extremes should thus be avoided in assessing the place of deliverance. On the one hand, one must take care not to overemphasize its importance. One of the devil's tactics is to present himself as more dangerous and more important than he is.[1] The focus should always be the Savior and our destiny of eternal life with him (cf. Lk 10:20). On the other hand, one must not limit God's design and his desire for all his children to receive the fullness of salvation, which includes liberation from evil. "If the Son makes you free, you will be free indeed" (Jn 8:36; cf. Lk 4:18). The liberation that we will enjoy fully in eternal life begins already in this life.

3.1.2   Deliverance and the Sacraments

Our liberation from evil is the work of God, who "wills that all men be saved and come to the knowledge of the truth" (1 Tim 2:4). "In many and various ways God spoke of old to our fathers by the prophets" (Heb 1:1), and when the fullness of time had come he sent his Son to redeem us and to adopt us as his sons and daughters (see Gal 1:4; 4:4-5). As Christ was sent forth by his Father in the power of the Holy Spirit, so he sent out his apostles:

This He did that, by preaching the gospel to every creature (Mk 16:15), they might proclaim that the Son of God, by His death and resurrection, had freed us from the power of Satan (Acts 26:18) and from death, and brought us into the kingdom of His Father. His purpose also was that they might accomplish the work of salvation which they had proclaimed, by means of sacrifice and sacraments.[2]

The Church continues to proclaim the good news of salvation accomplished in Christ's paschal mystery and to celebrate it in the liturgy and in the sacraments, which communicate his saving power. All the sacraments have a role in imparting the life of God to us and delivering us from evil, but three are especially efficacious against the devil: Baptism, Reconciliation, and the Eucharist.

Baptism saves us by plunging us into the passion and resurrection of Christ. Through Baptism we are liberated "from sin and from its instigator the devil" (CCC 1237) and are reborn as sons and daughters of God. We become members of Christ's body and temples of the Holy Spirit (CCC 1213, 1265), able to exercise the common priesthood by which we can offer our lives as a living sacrifice to God (cf. Rom 12:1). Baptism thus lays the foundation for all resistance to Satan during our pilgrimage in this life.

The sacrament of Reconciliation renews the gift of Baptism. By absolving us of sin it destroys one of the main avenues by which Satan tempts us and frightens us. By reconciling us with God and the Church, it strengthens us spiritually and offers us the support of the communion of saints. Frequent use of this sacrament helps us to keep locked those entryways by which the evil one has deceived and ensnared us.

Finally, the Eucharist has preeminence as "the supreme source of healing and liberation. Just as the sun dispels the darkness of night through the full force of its blazing light, Christ Jesus unfolds in the Eucharistic mystery all his power of life and victory over evil."[3] The Eucharist makes present the sacrifice by which Christ won victory over the devil: "As often as the sacrifice of the cross in which Christ our Passover was sacrificed, is celebrated on the altar, the work of our redemption is carried on."[4] It gives us the means for our daily spiritual combat by renewing and strengthening the grace received at Baptism, by purifying us and protecting us from sin, and by uniting us to Christ.

3.1.3 Deliverance and Evangelization

Deliverance from evil spirits finds its meaning not only as a part of God's work of salvation, but also as a sign of that salvation (cf. Mk 16:17). This is particularly true in the context of evangelization, which is the heart of the Church's mission.[5] Deliverance manifests the reality and efficacy of the good news as a saving power. Evangelization is not only about preaching the word of God but also about demonstrating that which the word announces: Christ has come to save us and is victorious over all evil. Throughout the New Testament, deliverance is one of the mighty deeds worked by Jesus and his disciples that bear witness to the gospel (cf. Lk 7:20-21; Acts 8:6-7). This is why Jesus sends his disciples out not only to preach, but also to heal and cast out demons (Lk 9:1-2; 10:1, 9, 17-19).

Just as some of Christ's healings are signs of his power to forgive (cf. Mk 2:1-12), so deliverance testifies to the heart of the gospel, "the beauty of the saving love of God made manifest in Jesus Christ who died and rose from the dead."[6] In this case what shines forth is God's power to liberate us and restore us to wholeness. Because deliverance is often intimate and hidden, it is mainly a sign for the person who receives it: it helps the delivered person believe in Christ's mercy and his authority over the forces of evil. But often it is a sign for those who witness it as well.

Deliverance is an eschatological sign: it reveals the kingdom of God, which is already present in a hidden way but still to come in its fullness. Being liberated from demonic power is an anticipation or foretaste of God's final victory over evil and the fullness of his sovereignty over all mankind, when Christ will have destroyed "every rule and every authority and every power" and God "will be all in all" (1 Cor 15:24, 28).

Deliverance thus plays a major role in the Church's primary mission of proclaiming the gospel. Already in parts of Africa and other regions of the world, deliverance ministry is central to Catholic evangelization. As a sign, deliverance finds its meaning in the wider context of witnessing to God's love and saving power.

3.2   Understanding Spiritual Bondage

To understand deliverance it is necessary to explain what we mean by spiritual bondage and oppression. This section and the next will address spiritual bondage; oppression will be treated in Section 3.4.

Most Christians have struggled at some moment in their lives, or maybe even quite frequently, with a difficulty that the regular practices of Christian life—confession and the Eucharist, a life of prayer, spiritual direction—are not able to alleviate. This difficulty may be, for instance, a repetitive sin, a strong negative emotion that wells up in certain situations, or a pattern of thought that becomes obsessive. However much we apply our will, these behaviors are almost impossible to resist and control. They are our first reaction and are so deeply ingrained that we might not even perceive them: we need a crisis or the help of others or the light of the Holy Spirit to do so.

Catholic tradition has developed a rich teaching on the ways in which demons can influence human beings, and how to combat them. Some authors, like the fifth-century monk St. John Cassian, speak about evil spirits taking "possession" of a person's mind and thoughts:

> It is clear then that unclean spirits cannot make their way into those whose bodies they are going to seize upon, in any other way than by first taking possession of their minds and thoughts.... It is a fact that those people are more grievously and severely troubled who, while they seem to be very little affected by them in the body, are yet possessed in spirit in a far worse way, as they are entangled in their sins and lusts. For as the apostle says, "whatever overcomes a man, to that he is enslaved" (2 Pet 2:19). Only in this respect they are more dangerously ill, because though they are the demons' slaves, yet they do not

know that they are assaulted by them, and under their dominion.[7]

For the desert Fathers, when a person gives in to temptation a process is set in motion that leads to "enslavement" or "captivity" of the soul. The seventh-century monk St. John Climacus explains:

> The discerning Fathers draw a distinction between attraction, liaison, consent, captivity, struggle, and what is called a passion of the soul…. Captivity is a forceful and involuntary abduction of the heart, or a permanent attachment to the object in question that destroys the good order of our soul…. They define passion in the proper sense as that which lurks disquietingly in the soul for a long time and through its intimacy with the soul brings it finally to what amounts to a habit, until the soul of its own accord clings to it with affection.[8]

Although one can fall into this state in the first place only if there is consent, the will becomes wounded and thus less able to resist temptation.[9] The conscience becomes dulled so it is quite difficult to recognize that a demon is at work.

The patristic teaching on spiritual combat is taken up and refined in the spiritual and mystical traditions of the Church. Dominican spirituality, for instance, following St. Thomas Aquinas,[10] has studied the ways demons can influence our imagination and thoughts. Ignatian spirituality offers wisdom on the ways the enemy harasses, tempts and deceives us, and on how to discern whether an interior movement comes from the enemy or from "the good spirit."[11] The Carmelite tradition and St. Francis de Sales describe how giving in to temptation produces a form of enslavement of the will.[12]

Spiritual bondage refers precisely to the kind of situation in which our will is to some degree bound or constrained, such that our conscience may not even perceive that something is amiss. The will is not fully destroyed, since it may be free in most situations. But it is impeded in some circumstances, so that its range of action is limited. For example, a woman may be peaceful and self-controlled most of the time, but underneath she is carrying deep-seated rage toward her mother, so that when she is with her mother she often loses control and ends up in a heated argument. In such a case, the will is present but unable to act; it is like a limb that is paralyzed but not amputated.

To understand what has just been described on a theological level, it is useful to compare spiritual bondage with other dimensions of evil related to our will, namely, sin and demon-possession. Seeing how it differs from these but also intersects with them will help us specify what spiritual bondage is, especially as the latter has been much less developed by theology. Two questions are at stake. First, what are the differences in the way the will is affected? Second, to what extent and in what way is there a demonic influence?

3.2.1 Spiritual Bondage in Relation to Sin

Human free will means that we are responsible for our acts, whether good or evil. Our will cannot be forced.[13] Even if a part of me does not want to commit a sin, if I do commit it, that means that on some level I did want it. Because of original sin, our will is weakened and inclined to evil; rather than being wholly set on what is good, it is often divided (cf. Ps 119:113).[14]

Sin and spiritual bondage seem quite similar, in that both involve the will. However, in the case of sin the will is *divided*, whereas with bondage the will is *constrained*. A divided will truly wants the sin it is committing, which is why the sinner is still to some extent free and responsible; but it also truly wants *not* to do it, which is why the person can fight against the sin. A constrained will, on the other hand, is practically unable to fight.

Spiritual bondage is very close to what traditional moral theology calls a "vice," a habit of sin created by repeating a particular sin. This strong tendency becomes extremely difficult to resist, as if the side of the divided will that inclines to the sin is so reinforced that the other side is almost helpless. "Everyone who commits sin is a slave to sin" (Jn 8:34). Although a vice is not the same as spiritual bondage, it would be a mistake to make too sharp a distinction between them, since in real life they overlap and reinforce each other.

What is the influence of the devil and demons in regard to sin? First, they are at the origin of some sins, since Genesis presents the serpent as the Tempter (Gen 3:1-6), at the source of original sin and thus indirectly of all sin. Some sins, even smaller sins, are the result of direct demonic temptation. However, temptation is only temptation: demons do not and cannot *cause* sin. Most theologians agree that they cannot directly influence our mind and will, but only our imagination, emotions, the material world around us, or in some cases, our bodies. They scare or deceive or tempt us into a choice, but this choice is ours. Moreover, direct demonic temptation is not a factor in every sin: the pull of disordered desires, the temptations of the flesh and the world are enough in many cases (cf. 1 Jn 2:16).[15]

But it is also true that sin always puts us under the dominion of the devil (CCC 407). Enslavement of the will is very often associated in Scripture with the influence of a demonic power: Jesus heals and frees those who are "under the authority of Satan" (Acts 26:18) or in the "snares" of the devil (2 Tim 2:26). In the same discourse in which Jesus speaks about being a slave to sin, he adds, "You are of your father the devil, and your will is to do your father's desires" (Jn 8:44). The presence of an exorcism during the rite of baptism testifies to the Church's conviction from ancient times that liberation from sin also means liberation from the devil. Nevertheless, in most cases the devil's dominion is only an exterior dominion. As sinners we do the devil's work (see Jn 8:41, 44) and thus conform ourselves to him, but his influence remains a moral influence.[16]

3.2.2 Spiritual Bondage in Relation to Possession

In some cases, however, the dominion is deeper. The New Testament describes persons who are possessed, or literally, "demonized" (*daimonizomenos*), which means they act under the influence of a demon. The person has lent himself, consciously or unconsciously, to an inner control that goes beyond the normal capacity of the forces of evil. The person has given demons a right that they do not possess in themselves. This is what happens in the case of what is traditionally called possession.

Spiritual bondage can best be understood as a milder form of this inner hold: an *influence* rather than control. Though there are degrees of both possession and spiritual bondage, and it is hard to draw a clear border between them, it is possible to distinguish between a form of control that touches the whole of the person and a partial influence, where the mind or will is impeded only in certain situations.

Just as demonic temptation is not a factor in all sins, but neither is it limited only to the most serious sins, so spiritual bondage should not be imagined to be everywhere, but neither should it be reserved to exceptional situations. Possession is a rare and extreme situation, while spiritual bondage, especially in its milder forms, may touch every aspect of life. This is why many traditions of Christian spirituality stress the spiritual combat, including the protection of guardian angels, the need to guard ourselves against the activity of demons, and the importance of discernment of spirits.

The way the devil works is multifaceted. We should approach these realities with humility, aware that they surpass our full comprehension. However, we believe that it is helpful to differentiate with more clarity these two different forms of demonic influence—spiritual bondage and possession—and thus help the Church in its pastoral care of souls. The better an enemy is known, the easier it is to fight it: "Put on the whole armor of God, that you may be able to stand against the wiles of the devil. For we are not contending against flesh and blood, but against the principalities, against the powers, against the world rulers of this present darkness, against the spiritual hosts of wickedness in the heavenly places" (Eph 6:11-12).

3.2.3   Types of Spiritual Bondage

Without seeking to be exhaustive, it may be helpful to specify some types of spiritual bondage.

A first type of bondage is that of overwhelming negative **emotions** such as guilt, fear, jealousy, despair, resentment, deep anger, rage, or hatred—sometimes directed toward a particular category of people, such as men or women, or authority figures.

Another type concerns repetitive and obsessive **thought patterns**. For instance, there may an attraction to death, or a habit of legalism, or a habit of interpreting the actions of others as an attack on oneself. This is sometimes related to a very specific sentence or word spoken to us in the past that has an inordinate amount of influence and power in our minds.

A third kind of bondage is **behavioral**: for instance, an irresistible urge to isolate oneself in difficult moments, or a constant need to control situations or people. Repetitive sins and compulsory temptations, as pornography or gambling or even lying, may fall into this category as well. In some cases addictions can be accompanied by a demonic influence.

Bondage may also be a possessive or unhealthy **relationship to a person**: one of our parents or siblings, a healer or seer, someone we are involved in a sinful activity with or have suffered from. In some cases the link exists with someone who is deceased.

An unhealthy or idolatrous **relation to objects** can be similar, whether because the object relates us to someone, or is particularly precious, or leads to obsessive behavior, or has an occult dimension.

In many cases bondage comes in clusters, for instance, jealousy, envy, suspicion and fear can open the door to and feed each other.

3.3   The Origin of Spiritual Bondage

Understanding the origin of a spiritual bondage helps the process of deliverance immensely. In most cases there is a combination of two factors. First there is a trauma or wound, or a psychological disorder, which gives a doorway or foothold to an evil spirit (cf. Eph 4:27). Second, there is a consent given by the person, which opens the door or allows the foothold to be used. Consent means that the person has on some level agreed to the demonic influence, even without doing so consciously. The fact that there is consent raises questions about the culpability of a demonized person, the possibility of "taking back" consent, and to what extent there can be consent in the case of small children or groups of people. These will be discussed below.

3.3.1   *What Gives a Foothold to Demons*

The point of entrance for evil spirits can be specified in three types, on a scale of increasing severity.

The lowest degree is **wounds and traumas**. These can be a painful event or series of events (such as a negative judgment by a parent or teacher), especially in the earlier years of life when a person is the most sensitive and prone to be influenced. Even the circumstances of conception and birth may have powerful effects, especially in the case of a rape or an extramarital relationship, when the child is not wanted or when the mother has experienced great fear. Sometimes a wound does not come from a specific event but from a familial or social environment—for example, a violent or distrustful family, a country at war, or a country that has experienced political oppression, apartheid, or tyranny. For the most part, the real difficulty is not the circumstances themselves but the way they are experienced and understood. People may experience the same ordinary or extremely severe situations and yet react very differently; some are traumatized, while others are not. The inner wound created in this way leads the person to seek protection, consolation, or compensation. For instance, when one has suffered violence, one may respond with isolation or with violence in return. These emotional and behavioral patterns offer an entryway for demons, which infest the weakness by inflaming it. A spirit can reinforce the pattern, and in doing so it takes hold of that area of the person's inner life.

A second type of foothold for demonic forces is **sins**. Repeated sins—especially unrepented ones—create a habit of sin and weaken the will in that specific area, to the point that it can more easily be taken over by an evil spirit. Spiritual bondage then reinforces the orientation of the will toward the sin, to the point where it is incapable of choosing any other: it is not merely divided but constrained (bound). Even sins of omission, such as the refusal to forgive, can be in this category. Extreme sins committed against vulnerable people, such as torture, rape, warfare, abortion—or even milder sins against the defenseless—also open doors to evil spirits because they dispose the person to choose evil.

In some cases, sin is not personal but embedded in social structures, whether familial (for instance, a pattern of anger, or incest) or ethnic or national (slavery, racism, colonization, war). People are less culpable for structures of sin than for personal sins, because there is a lesser degree of voluntary choice. However, precisely for this reason, structures of sin are more difficult to recognize as sins and are often less resisted. They may be so closely knitted into a person's identity that he or she gives them free reign and absolutely refuses to reject them. So they too offer entry points to evil spirits.

The third and most serious kind of foothold for the demonic is **occult practices**, which have become alarmingly common, even among Catholics. These range from an occasional participation in the occult to pacts with the devil.[17] In some cases the contact with the occult comes through the family. Some practices from pagan religions are also in this category, as are false private revelations and any form of idolatry. Extreme involvement in an ideology or a "cause" (such as radical political commitments or nationalism or legalism), although not directly occult, can be idolatrous, because it is an attempt to save the world and oneself through our own strength. All of these offer the easiest entryways for demonic forces, because they are explicitly or implicitly related to them already. This is why Scripture strongly condemns these practices (Dt 18:10-11). Turning to the occult means asking help from evil spirits, and this relationship invites them into our lives.

In all three cases there is a vicious circle. Wounds open the way to spiritual bondage, but the bondage keeps the wound open and does not allow it to heal. Paradoxically, the negative emotional or cognitive or behavioral pattern, although chosen as a protection, actually hurts the person even more. For instance, isolation or revenge in response to violence cuts the person off from others even more. Sin opens a door to spiritual bondage, but bondage also generates the sin by reinforcing it and turning it into a kind of second nature.

All this means that deliverance is closely related to both inner healing and repentance from sin. Deliverance, healing and repentance cannot be separated, since it is useless to renounce and expel an evil spirit if its foothold is still available.

3.3.2 Spiritual Bondage in Relation to Psychological Troubles

Another entry point for spiritual bondage can be psychological troubles. This entry point is different from the others because it is often difficult to distinguish between spiritual bondage and psychological disorders. Their symptoms can be quite similar. Just as grace presupposes nature and manifests itself through nature, demonic influence affects nature and expresses itself through psychological, emotional and mental symptoms. Moreover, in some cases there may be a vicious circle: mental illness can offer a foothold for demonization, while evil spirits may reinforce the emotional distress or obsessive thoughts or behavior patterns.

There is true difference, however, and neither can be reduced to the other. Psychological disorders are more intertwined with a person's psyche and identity, and thus are more continuous and lasting. They originate from the fragility of nature rather than from demonic forces. The Church has a long tradition of distinguishing between demonic affliction and mental illness. For example, by insisting on discernment before the rite of exorcism is carried out, the Church testifies to both the outward similarity and the true difference in nature between them.[18] Jesus' ministry shows that outwardly similar ailments can be of either natural origin or demonic origin: sometimes the blind, mute or deaf are simply healed (Mt 15:30; 20:29-34; Mk 7:31-37), while in other instances a spirit needs to be cast out (Mt 9:32-34; 12:22; Mk 9:14-29).

Because of this difference in nature, before doing deliverance it is essential to discern what type of trouble the person is suffering from, with the help of a professional when necessary. Treating a psychological trouble as if it were spiritual may actually open the way for spiritual bondage, while treating a spiritual bondage as if it were merely psychological is ineffective and frustrating.

Without claiming to be exhaustive, it is possible to offer two criteria of discernment. First, psychological disorders are often more deeply rooted in a person's psyche and identity; they sometimes affect the structure of the personality, whereas spiritual bondage tends to affect a more limited area of the person's life. Second, spiritual bondage may intensify when the person is turning to God and seeking to grow in virtue. For instance, a spirit of idolatry will try to turn the person away from participating in sacraments. Some psychological disorders, on the other hand, may push the person toward a more active religious life.

Because of the similarity of symptoms and the interrelation between spiritual bondage and psychological trouble, distinguishing between them is not always an either/or process. Additionally, some people refuse the true nature of their disorder: some resist the fact that they are mentally ill and develop "demonopathy"—that is, they attribute all ailments to demons. Others refuse to recognize the existence of the spiritual world. Discernment requires prudence, wisdom and experience.

3.3.3   Acceptance of a Lie

A foothold is not in itself enough to produce spiritual bondage. Since no one can directly influence our mind and will other than God and ourselves, spiritual bondage can only occur insofar as a person gives consent. Consent opens the entryway that is otherwise inaccessible for any evil spirit.

Consent is not necessarily a fully conscious process. Sometimes it simply means the person embraces a judgment, however troubling, because it seems overbearingly true. After hearing a parent or an authority figure repeat that you are good for nothing, you will not want it to be true, but may feel compelled to believe it is true. In most cases, the person is not consenting directly to the evil spirit but to a behavioral pattern that protects, comforts, or numbs their pain. Going up the scale of types of demonic footholds, from wounds to sins to the occult, the act of consent becomes more explicit and direct.

What is consented to in such cases is always a lie: the person agrees to and identifies with a deception. As children of God, we are to "live by every word that comes from the mouth of God" (Mt 4:4), that is, we live by the truth God reveals to us: we are created "in his image and likeness" (Gen 1:26-27), we are "precious in [his] eyes" (Isa 43:4), we are "his work of art" (Eph 2:10). One of the main titles of Satan, on the other hand, is "father of lies" (Jn 8:44), since his influence is always fueled by a lie. The lie can be about God's love, kindness and power, about ourselves and our worth, or about others and their attitude towards us. For example, a child whose father abandoned the family may feel a sense of rejection and at a deep level may believe lies such as these: "I am not worthy to be loved. I will always be rejected. God is remote and unconcerned about me." Or a child who experienced harsh discipline or an emotionally distant parent may believe, "My value is based on what I achieve. I will always be a failure. I will never be able to change. God is a hard taskmaster always focused on what I do wrong."

We have, then, the option to believe God's word and form our sense of self according to his word, or to consent to the lie and allow the lie to bind us and rob us of inner peace and joy. In the latter case, at a subconscious level these lies become deeply rooted in our heart, influencing our thoughts and actions. They become inner "strongholds" (cf. 2 Cor 10:4)—systems of faulty thinking by which the evil one is able to manipulate and enslave us. This can be the case even if at a conscious level one has embraced the truth of the gospel. Instead of thinking and acting out of a deep confidence in God, one is driven by compulsions that are rooted in these inner wounds and lies.

The role of consent raises the question of the degree to which a demonized person is culpable in the process that leads to his loss of freedom. Spiritual bondage always involves some personal responsibility, an act of consent sufficient to give evil spirits a "right" to influence our will. However, because of the foothold and the deception, the degree of voluntary involvement may be minimal. There are often strong mitigating factors, which means that the demonized person may be more of a sufferer than a guilty party. God alone can judge the degree of a person's culpability. Neither the deliverance minister nor the afflicted person should attempt to do so (cf. 1 Cor 4:4).

The role of consent also raises the question, is it not possible simply to take back one's consent? In theory it is possible. However, consent is more than a fleeting agreement; it always contains an element of permanency: our free will has a mysterious capacity to promise and commit.[19] We not only choose our present, but to a certain extent our future as well. This ability to give consent is a beautiful gift—the key to faithful love of God and of others—but it is fraught with danger, because it can also become the source of the worst perversions. Because of this, withdrawing our consent normally requires an explicit and deliberate act of renunciation. Without consent there can be no bondage, and without renunciation there can be no deliverance.

3.3.4 Spiritual Bondage in Children or Groups of People

What about types of spiritual bondage that seem to take hold without personal consent, such as those that affect a child or a group of people?

The case of children who seem to contract spiritual bondage before the age of reason, which means before they are able to fully exercise free will, derives from the profound influence that parents and other adults have on the children entrusted to them. Scripture speaks of God "visiting the iniquity of the fathers upon the children to the third and the fourth generation of those who hate me" (Ex 20:5). This intergenerational influence is not to be understood as the parents' *guilt* being passed on to their children, but rather the *consequences* of their sins, including spiritual bondage. The spiritual authority that parents have over their children is what enables them to say "yes" for them at their baptism, but conversely, also enables them to open the door to evil influences. Yet just as God's grace is fully effective only if it is personally ratified, so a spiritual bondage attains its negative influence only if it is ratified as a child grows more capable of conscious personal choice. The ties that connect a child to its family and society open the way for an influence of spiritual forces on the child's emotions and imagination, and make it more difficult not to consent, but in the end spiritual bondage always implies there is a form of consent. The varied responses of children to similar circumstances are a mystery that involves freedom, grace, temperament, and the natural and spiritual environment that parents provide.

In some cases, spiritual bondage can touch a group, whether a family, an ethnic group, or a nation. For instance, one ethnic group can have a deeply ingrained prejudice against another. For each individual born into the group, besides the obvious cultural influence, the deep ties that bind a group together are also at work to transmit a spiritual influence (in this case, an evil influence). However, it becomes a spiritual bondage in the individual only to the degree he or she personally ratifies it. We know too well how difficult it is to refuse consent to values and emotions inherited from our family or nation, but it is possible.

3.4 Understanding Oppression

A lesser form of demonic influence than spiritual bondage, but one that can still cause great suffering, is oppression. Though one should not exaggerate the distinction between bondage and oppression, because they often tend to overlap in real life and the one easily slides into the other, the most fundamental difference is that oppression does not necessarily involve consent. This means that it is less interior: it consists in physical or emotional harassment, or obsessive thoughts, but the will is not directly constrained.

How can there be a demonic influence without consent? As noted in Section 3.2.1, though demonic powers cannot directly act on a person's will, they can touch the body, the emotions and the imagination.[20] Through the fear, despair or other emotions induced, thoughts may be generated and decisions made that may give the impression that the will is controlled, but in fact it is only indirectly influenced.

3.4.1 Causes of Demonic Oppression

What then explains why some people suffer oppression and others not? As with suffering in general, we must admit that we are in front of a mystery and that not all can be understood. As in the case of the fallen tower of Siloam (Lk 13:4), there is no fault or sin that conveniently explains the suffering of the innocent. Some people are more exposed to oppression than others for different reasons: some because of great spiritual progress and fruitfulness, which the demons would like to obstruct; others because of psychological fragility (see Section 3.3.2). A culture that stresses the activity of evil spirits may open the way to oppression through an exaggerated fear of their power—but, paradoxically, a culture that denies evil spirits will render people vulnerable as well, because the enemy is not recognized.

3.4.2   Curses and Spells

Sometimes the origin of oppression is another person, as in the case of curses or spells.[21] These are considered superstition in some modern cultures, but are seen as obviously real in so many traditional cultures that they cannot be dismissed without reflection. The Bible contains a remarkable number of blessings (410) and curses (230).[22] Jesus himself cursed the fig tree (cf. Mt 21:19), and St. Paul's letters make it clear that he takes curses seriously enough to ban them (Rom 12:14). What then allows someone to direct demonic forces towards a fellow human being in this way?

To understand this, we should consider the numerous ties through which human beings relate to each other and constantly exert influence on each other. We usually think of these ties on a psychological and cultural level, but they may also exist on a deeper, less perceptible, metaphysical level. This conviction set the framework for the way the Fathers of the Church understood salvation in Jesus Christ, which spreads out to all through the deep link Christ has with all humanity through his incarnation.[23] Of course, God strengthens these bonds and forms a unified people of God, through which we become one body in Christ and thus "members of one another" (Rom 12:5; cf. 1 Cor 12:27). Modern thought has brought a great gift by underlining the importance of the individual, but it is time to retrieve the wealth still present in traditional cultures, which understand the individual as always inserted into a greater whole that precedes him or her. These deep ties afford the background for the power and effectiveness of words. Words not only reflect reality, but also shape it, for good and for evil.[24]

The way all human beings are interwoven with one another allows for the circulation of grace, but also of evil influences; this is one of the ways of understanding how original sin was spread from Adam to the rest of humanity. Demonic forces can also ride on these human ties, so to speak, when someone puts a curse or spell on someone else. It is sometimes said that curses are particularly effective when pronounced by a relative: this seems quite reasonable, because the links between members of a family are even closer than with the rest of humanity.

We must not imagine that people invoking evil spirits over others actually have mastery over these spirits. In fact it is the reverse: whoever has recourse to evil spirits by pronouncing a curse or casting a spell is progressively taken control of by those spirits.

After reflecting on the distinction between oppression and bondage, it is important to stress once again how easily one can slip into the other. A person may consent to the emotions and thoughts brought on by demonic harassment, or can react with other self-protective patterns that lead to bondage, just as in the case of wounds (see Section 3.3.1).

Every believer has a responsibility to stand firm in faith, to resist and not to submit to the fear aroused by those who invoke evil spirits (1 Cor 16:13; 1 Pet 5:8-9).

3.5 Understanding Deliverance Ministry

Because of the differences between sin on the one hand and spiritual bondage and oppression on the other, the process by which freedom is restored also differs. Sin requires repentance—a conversion (*metanoia*) of our will away from sin and toward God—and forgiveness. Spiritual bondage and oppression, on the other hand, require deliverance.

The term "deliverance" is not the only possible term, but it has become customary and is quite appropriate. It helps us distinguish the process from major exorcism. It also recalls that deliverance from evil spirits finds its meaning in relation to the whole of salvation, which is also called "deliverance." Deliverance from slavery is the foundational salvific experience of the people of Israel, narrated in Exodus and recalled throughout the Scriptures. "Deliverance" stresses the fact that we are freed from a force that constrains and enslaves us. Christ came to "deliver all those who through fear of death were subject to lifelong slavery" (Heb 2:15; see Col 1:13-14; Ps 107:13).

It should be noted that deliverance ministry is not always necessary to recover freedom. Sometimes simply the spiritual growth of the person, his or her recourse to regular prayer and Scripture reading, participation in the liturgy and sacraments, and living a good moral life will suffice. The Eucharist and the sacrament of Reconciliation in particular, because they free us from sins and renew our communion with God and the Church, are powerful means of being freed from the devil's influence. This is especially the case when the foothold for demonic influence is a wound: if there is inner healing and growth in holiness, the evil spirit loses a place to dwell. A Christian is never alone, and the support of a Christian community and the mediation of the Church is invaluable.

3.5.1 Baptismal Authority over the Powers of Evil

Our capacity to pray for deliverance comes from the authority we have been given by Christ. It is Christ who has absolute authority over the realm of darkness, demonstrated during his public ministry by his confrontations with evil spirits and his exorcisms. This authority is won by his passion and resurrection, which complete his victory over Satan: "He disarmed the rulers and authorities and put them to open shame by triumphing over them" (Col 2:15). As Christians we share in Christ's authority over the powers of darkness.

The theological virtues of faith, hope and charity, given to us by the Holy Spirit in baptism, confer on us the strength to reject Satan in our lives. Receiving freedom entails the ability to hold onto that freedom, protect it, and make it grow (cf. Gal 5:1). This fight is part of our daily life, as expressed by the Lord's Prayer: "deliver us from the evil one," and by the many New Testament exhortations to stand fast against the evil one (Eph 6:10-17; Jas 4:7; 1 Pet 5:9). As noted in Section 2.4, this authority has also been entrusted to all disciples to help others (Mk 16:17; Lk 10:17-20).

Practicing deliverance ministry thus does not imply any new gift or mission, but simply taking hold of and putting into action the freedom and the authority Christ has given us, for ourselves and for others. We are already in the kingdom of God, though its fullness is still to come, and we are to embrace this reality in full confidence and faith.

Two of the key elements of deliverance are renunciation and direct commands. It is important to understand why these are needed and why they are effective through the authority given to us by Christ.

3.5.2   The Efficacy of Renunciation

The first expression of this freedom and authority Christ has given us is renouncing the devil, his works, and his footholds in our life. Renunciation is an important part of deliverance because of the major role played by consent in contracting spiritual bondage (and the porous boundary between oppression and spiritual bondage). Renouncing the bondage and the demonic force behind it closes the door we have opened through our free will. It should be done explicitly, aloud and with full sincerity, to overturn the commitment we made in consenting to a lie (whether it was conscious or unconscious).

Renunciation is truly effective for two reasons: first, simply because of the natural ability of the will, the same will by which we originally gave consent; second, and even more so, because of the freedom and authority Christ has given us to fight the evil one in our own life in his name.

3.5.3   The Role of Direct Commands

Another central element of deliverance is to adjure the evil spirit, that is, to command it in the name of God or Jesus.[25] Adjuration is "the invocation of God, or a holy thing, or one of the saints for the purpose of inducing someone to do or to omit something."[26] In the case of deliverance, this means one invokes the name of Jesus to command the spirit to stop afflicting the person and to leave. This is part of deliverance because it is the way Jesus and his disciples cast out demons, and has been taken up by the Church. It is usually not enough simply to take back our consent to a lie, because we are not dealing only with ourselves, but with another being.

Here too, we are simply putting into action the authority God has given us over evil spirits in our lives and in the lives of others, which is recognized in Catholic tradition. St. Thomas Aquinas wrote, "It is written (Mark 16:17): 'In My name they shall cast out devils.' Now to induce anyone to do a certain thing for the sake of God's name is to adjure. Therefore it is lawful to adjure the demons."[27] As an exercise of our God-given authority, adjuration is legitimate and effective.

Commanding a spirit to leave should generally be done only *after* the afflicted person has renounced those things that gave an entryway to demonic influence in the first place (3.5.2). Otherwise evil spirits still have a right of access to the person, and the command may bring temporary relief without lasting freedom.

3.5.4 The Limitations of Deliverance Ministry

Although deliverance ministry is truly efficacious, it is important to keep in mind that it is not a sacrament or a sacramental.[28] The Catholic faith holds that the seven sacraments are efficacious by the very fact of being celebrated, apart from any human dispositions. "The sacrament is not wrought by the righteousness of either the celebrant or the recipient, but by the power of God" (St. Thomas Aquinas, quoted in CCC 1128). However, receiving the full fruits of the sacrament depends on a disposition of faith. In a similar way, sacramentals are efficacious through the prayers and holiness of the Church, although here too a disposition of faith is needed.[29]

Deliverance ministry is like sacraments and sacramentals in that its ultimate source is Christ's saving power and overflowing grace available to us through the Church. But it is unlike sacraments and sacramentals in that the Church does not commit itself by institutionalizing a practice through a rite. What is most decisive is the faith and moral integrity of the deliverance minister and (in cases of spiritual bondage, where there has been consent) the afflicted person's freely renouncing the demonic hold and choosing to allow Christ to reign in his life.

4

Exorcism and Deliverance in Church History

They went forth and preached everywhere, while the Lord worked with them and confirmed the message by the signs that attended it.

– Mark 16:20

A look at the history of the Church will help us understand the important place that combat against demons has had in the ministry of the Church and the spiritual life of the faithful. It will also enable us to consider the Church's understanding of the role of the laity in this ministry.

4.1   Exorcism in Patristic Writings

The testimonies that have come down from the early centuries indicate that the casting out of demons remained an ordinary part of the life of the Church, as it had been in the apostolic era. This is true especially in evangelistic contexts. In fact, deliverances, along with healings and miracles, were a major factor in the exponential growth of the Church in the first four centuries.[1] The casting out of demons by Christians was so frequent and well known that St. Justin Martyr (c.

100-165 AD) could speak of it as irrefutable evidence for the truth of the gospel. In his *Second Apology*, addressed to the Roman Senate, Justin wrote,

> Jesus was born by the will of God the Father for the salvation of believers and the destruction of demons. And now you can learn this by what you see with your own eyes. For throughout the whole world and in your city there are many demoniacs whom all the other exorcists, sorcerers and magicians could not heal, but whom our Christians have healed and do heal, disabling and casting out the demons who possessed them in the name of Jesus Christ who was crucified under Pontius Pilate.[2]

St. Irenaeus (c. 115-202) likewise spoke of deliverance and other supernatural works done by Christians as a leading cause of the conversion of many to Christ:

> Those who are in truth his disciples, receiving grace from him, perform miracles in his name so as to promote the welfare of others, according to the gift which each one has received from him. For some do certainly and truly drive out devils, so that frequently those who have been cleansed from evil spirits both believe in Christ and join themselves to the Church. Others have foreknowledge of things to come: they see visions and utter prophecies. Still others heal the sick by laying their hands upon them, and they are made whole. Yes, moreover, the dead have even been raised up, and remained among us for many years.[3]

Tertullian (c. 155 – c. 240), seeking to convince his contemporaries that the Christian life is far nobler and more enjoyable than the pagan life, asks, "What nobler than to tread underfoot the gods of the nations, to exorcise evil spirits, to perform cures, to seek divine revelations, to live to God? These are the pleasures, these the spectacles that befit Christians."[4]

What other exorcists did by formulas, spells, and incantations, Christians did simply by faith in the name of Jesus. It was not only the ordained but also lay believers who did these works of power as they spread the gospel. As Origen (c. 185-253) points out, Christ's grace is all the more manifest when miracles are done in his name by the simplest of people. Christians cast out demons, he said,

> without the use of any curious arts of magic, or incantations, but merely by prayer and simple adjurations which the plainest person can use. Because for the most part it is uneducated persons who perform this work, thus making manifest the grace that is in the word of Christ and the despicable weakness of demons, which, in order to be overcome and driven out of the bodies and souls of men, do not require the power and wisdom of those who are mighty in argument or most learned in matters of faith.[5]

St. Cyprian of Carthage (d. 258), in recounting to a friend what occurred at his baptism, describes the spiritual power bestowed by the Holy Spirit on those who receive this sacrament—another witness to the fact that power over evil was considered a gift received by all Christians:

God pours out his Spirit without measure.... By that grace we are given power in all purity to heal the sick, whether of body or mind, to reconcile enemies, to quell violence, to calm passions, to reprimand demons and force them to disclose their identity, punishing them with sharp blows until, with loud shrieks and struggles, they flee in terror. The blows we deal them are invisible, but what they effect is manifest to all.... How tremendous is this freedom and the spiritual power the Lord has given us! Not only are we protected from harm, but we are given authority over the whole force of the enemy who attacks us![6]

St. Hilary of Poitiers (c. 300-368) likewise mentions authority over demons as an effect of baptism:

We who have been reborn through the sacrament of baptism experience intense joy when we feel within us the first stirrings of the Holy Spirit. We begin to have insight into the mysteries of faith; we are able to prophesy and speak with wisdom. We become steadfast in hope and receive abundant gifts of healing. Demons are made subject to our authority. These gifts enter us as a gentle rain. Little by little they bear abundant fruit.[7]

These early testimonies show that the ability of Christ's disciples to liberate people from demons was experienced as a new and astonishing phenomenon in the ancient world, plagued as it was by idolatry, immorality, and various forms of spiritual bondage. Through these works of deliverance the oppressed were being set free and the name of Jesus was being exalted among the nations.

4.2   Gradual Regulation of the Practice of Exorcism

During the subsequent centuries the Church gradually regulated the practice of casting out demons, as she did for many other practices. This was a wise pastoral reaction to certain abuses, but also, more positively, an expression of the desire of the Church to institutionalize the ministry of deliverance and place the full weight of its spiritual authority behind it.

The first rules appear in the context of both exorcising the possessed (called *energumens*) and preparation for baptism, during which exorcisms were performed over all the catechumens to free them from any demonic influence.[8] Documents from the middle of the third century show that exorcists were a defined group within the Church.[9] Eventually the Western Church created an order of exorcists, i.e., of those ordained for the ministry of exorcism.[10] In subsequent centuries exorcisms were usually reserved to these exorcists (and to priests and bishops), but the Church still held that those with a charism of exorcism could cast out demons even if they were not ordained for it. In the Eastern Church, exorcism remained a charismatic function not tied to ordination.[11]

During the Middle Ages the order of exorcist became one of the minor orders on the way to priesthood. The usual minister of exorcisms became the bishop or a priest, although others could exorcise in exceptional situations.[12] From the *Roman Ritual* of 1614 it became a universal practice that only those given permission by their bishop could perform exorcisms,[13] and finally, the Code of Canon Law of 1917 reserved exorcisms solely to priests and bishops.[14] Similarly, the way of performing exorcisms was progressively institutionalized: the first standard formulas appeared in the West in the eighth century, and in the seventeenth century the *Roman Ritual* promulgated (but did not mandate) the first official rite of exorcism.[15]

In the meantime, more clarity grew about a diversity of ways of casting out demons. The type reserved to ordained ministers and invested with the authority of the Church was named "public," since it is performed in the name of the Church with a precise ritual. However, moral theologians in the modern period also developed the notion of a "private" exorcism for less severe cases of demonic influence. St. Alphonsus Liguori noted that these private exorcisms are not reserved to priests or bishops and need no special authorization, but are "permissible to all."[16] Some moralists stress that they are to be used frequently.[17] They are commended to all confessors, as well as to each of the faithful for their own spiritual life. In some cases, especially if they have the charismatic gift of miracles, the faithful perform private exorcisms to free someone other than themselves.[18] The regulation of combat against demons by the Church thus leaves open a space for all the faithful to take their part.

4.3 Canon Law

The present Code of Canon Law has provisions only for exorcism "on the possessed [*in obsessos*]" (canon 1172). The Code stipulates that these must be practiced by a priest, with explicit and special permission of the bishop. Such an exorcism is a sacramental (CCC 1673).

Authorized commentaries specify that these provisions concern only solemn or major exorcisms, i.e., public exorcisms that are not part of another rite.[19] They do not concern minor exorcisms, which are public but are part of another rite such as the catechumenate or baptism, and can be practiced by the minister who has the power to celebrate the given rite. Nor do they concern private exorcisms: there are no provisions for these in the Code.

4.4 A Vatican Document of 1985

In 1985 the Congregation for the Doctrine of the Faith issued a document with some more details, *Letter to Ordinaries Regarding Norms on Exorcism* (*Inde ab aliquot*). The Congregation was asked to give its opinion on prayer groups in the Church led by lay people where deliverance from demons is practiced, even when these are not properly speaking exorcisms. A first comment to be made is that the Congregation thus recognizes that some people practice a form of deliverance which is not exorcism, that lay people lead these, and that neither of these is forbidden.

The document makes three points. First, Canon Law must be observed, especially the provision that exorcisms may only be performed by priests with the explicit permission of the bishop (canon 1172). Second, laypersons may not use the prayer of Exorcism of Satan and the Fallen Angels published under the authority of Pope Leo XIII.[20] Third, the document stresses that, even in the more general case of deliverance from demonic influence (rather than full exorcism), public meetings in which demons are "questioned directly and their identities sought to be known" by "those who are without the due faculty" are not permitted. Finally the document recommends that the faithful pray to be protected from evil according to the words of the Lord's prayer, "deliver us from evil" (Mt 6:13) and advises recourse to the sacraments and to the intercession of Mary, the angels and the saints.

A widespread interpretation of the third point holds that it prohibits lay people from giving direct commands to demons. We do not believe this to be the correct understanding.

First, this point does not concern only laypersons but anyone who has not received explicit permission from the bishop, so priests also fall into this category. Second, the Latin original states that demons should not be "questioned directly" (*directe interpellantur*).[21] This does not correspond to a prohibition of direct command but rather of dialogue with demons. The rest of the sentence—"questioned directly and their identities sought to be known"—confirms this understanding. Though it is not exclusive, there is a strong link between *interpellare* and seeking the spirit's identity: demons should *especially* not be questioned with the intention of seeking their names.

For these reasons, we understand that *Inde ab aliquot* forbids anyone, layperson or priest, who has not received authorization to practice public exorcisms from the bishop, to dialogue with demons, to ask them for help, and especially to question them about their identity. Though it does not commend any other form of direct address or confrontation with demons, it does not prohibit them either—so it does not prohibit direct commands spoken by the lay faithful.

4.5 Conclusion

This brief review of the practice of deliverance from demonic influence in the history of the Church shows that at all times she has offered protection and active defense against demonic oppression and bondage, in the context of evangelization, during the catechumenate, or simply as part of the spiritual care of the faithful. Wisely, the Church has imposed order and discipline on this practice and committed her authority to it, gradually restricting the rite of exorcism to bishops and to priests who receive the legitimate authorization. However, these regulations concern almost exclusively what we now call major exorcisms, for those who are possessed. Deliverance from the more general influence of demonic forces has not been regulated in the same way and is open to all priests and to the faithful.

5

Pastoral Guidelines

*The people gathered..., bringing the sick and those afflicted
with unclean spirits, and they were all healed.*

– Acts 5:16

Through the growth of deliverance ministries in recent decades the Lord has been restoring a dimension of the Church's mission that had long been neglected. Deliverance from demonic oppression has become once again a prominent sign accompanying the Christian witness to the gospel, visibly manifesting the reality of the kingdom (cf. Mk 16:17-20). Through the faith and prayer of ordinary believers, countless people have existentially experienced Christ's victory over evil and his power to set captives free. Deliverance ministry has thus become an important component of the new evangelization.

As the need for deliverance continues to grow, among Christians as well as non-Christians, so does the need for prudent oversight on the part of the pastors of the Church. In accord with St. Paul's instruction, "Do not quench the Spirit, ... but test everything; hold fast what is good, abstain from every form of evil" (1 Thess 5:19-22), the purpose of pastoral oversight is not to hinder deliverance ministry but to ensure that it is carried out in a responsible way and in full accord with Catholic faith. This chapter offers some general guidelines, without attempting to describe or prescribe any one method of deliverance ministry.[1] These guidelines may need to be adapted for particular cultural or ecclesial contexts.

5.1 Who Can Do Deliverance Ministry?

As noted in Sections 2.4 and 4.1, Scripture and Catholic tradition have always recognized that deliverance (what was traditionally called simple exorcism) can be done by lay people as well as priests. It does not follow, however, that all believers should be involved in deliverance ministry. There are varying levels of involvement in deliverance, and there is need for pastoral wisdom and common sense in discerning who should be involved.

5.1.1 Self-Deliverance

Deliverance on the most basic level consists in the effort to free *oneself* from the influence of Satan. All Christians can and should engage in this effort any time they experience temptation or sense that they are under some form of demonic oppression or bondage. One simple way of doing so is by praying as Jesus taught us, "Deliver us from evil." As the Catechism teaches, this petition of the Our Father is a prayer for protection from Satan, the Evil One, who seeks to disrupt and destroy God's work of salvation in Christ (CCC, 2850). It is good to pray the Our Father frequently, along with other traditional prayers such as the Rosary and the prayer to St.

Michael the Archangel, as well as spontaneous prayers in our own words, speaking as children to our heavenly Father. Prayer in tongues is also an effective means of repelling the influence of evil spirits. Another way of combatting the enemy is by commanding demons to leave in the name of Jesus. Such commands should be spoken with confident trust in the Lord, and accompanied by prayer to him.

Self-deliverance should always be done in the context of other forms of protection from evil, including regular practice of the sacraments, daily prayer and Scripture reading, putting off habits of sin, and participation in a Christian faith-sharing community or small group.

5.1.2   *Occasional Deliverance for Others*

Second, deliverance consists in helping *another person* break free of demonic oppression or bondage, through either prayer to God or direct commands to demons. Anyone who is living a mature Christian life can do deliverance in this sense for family members, friends, members of their prayer group, or occasionally for others such as a person they are evangelizing. Deliverance in this sense is done in an informal way and should be accompanied by an explanation that helps the other person draw closer to Jesus and place their trust in him.

5.1.3   *Deliverance as a Ministry*

Finally, some people are called to deliverance as a *ministry*, in which they practice deliverance on a regular basis and for people whom they do not know personally. Such ministries are accountable to the proper Church authority, usually either the local bishop (sometimes via the diocesan leaders of the Catholic Charismatic Renewal) or the pastor. Accountability to higher authority is an important safeguard for those involved in deliverance, as in any area of ministry. The decision to be involved in deliverance ministry is not one that can be made on one's own, but only with the guidance of wise spiritual advisers and those in authority. It is very easy to have a higher opinion of our knowledge and abilities than is warranted. In fact, some of those who are most convinced they should be involved in deliverance ministry are those least suitable for it.

All deliverance ministries should carefully screen and select their team members. Those invited onto the team should be persons of Christian maturity, psychological health, holiness of life, humility, and docility to ecclesial authority. They must be free of any serious sin and of hidden self-centered motives such as pride or a desire for attention. They must be faithful in the regular practices of the Christian life, including daily prayer and Scripture reading, regular recourse to the Eucharist and the sacrament of Reconciliation, and growth in virtue. In addition to their accountability to the ministry leadership, they should also be accountable to a spiritual director or a Christian faith-sharing group who will be honest in calling them to task when necessary. Finally, before doing deliverance ministry themselves they should receive training and gain experience with the help of others who are more experienced.

Catholic tradition recognizes that some people, both men and women, have a special charism of deliverance or exorcism.[2] This gift is often understood as one form of the charism of "mighty deeds" mentioned by Paul. It is often joined to the charism of discernment of spirits (see Section 5.2.1), which gives a person special insight as to what kinds of demons are operating in a particular situation and how to deal with them. Lay people who have these charisms are often invited by diocesan exorcists to collaborate in the ministry of exorcism as well as deliverance—an example of fruitful cooperation between clergy and laity. Although the charism is not essential for deliverance ministry (just as one does not need a charism of healing to pray for healing), persons with the charism are especially effective in the ministry. Often the charism will arise and develop precisely through practice.

All deliverance ministries must ensure that their team members receive adequate training and continued oversight. From time to time the leaders should seek feedback from people who received ministry, to find out whether they were helped by it and whether they were treated with love and respect.

5.2 When Is It Appropriate to Do Deliverance Ministry?

Before doing deliverance ministry it is necessary first to discern whether a person needs deliverance as opposed to some other kind of ministry. This is not always a simple matter, since demons are purely spiritual beings that cannot be observed empirically. Their presence can be difficult to detect. Moreover, demons are deceitful, often seeking to camouflage their presence and activity. Some of the symptoms of their activity are deceptively similar to symptoms of mental illness. It is a mistake, however, to separate illness and demonic oppression too strictly (see Section 3.3.2). As the Gospels and contemporary experience demonstrate, very often people have a *combined* need for healing and deliverance. The following criteria are helpful in discernment.

5.2.1 When Deliverance Ministry Is Appropriate

There are several signs that indicate a person's need for deliverance ministry.

o **The afflicted person's own sense that evil spirits may be involved.** Often a person is aware of an influence of evil that goes beyond what can be explained by emotional or psychological factors. For example, a person may experience evil in the form of frequent blasphemous thoughts during Mass; or unusually frightening nightmares or visions of evil; or inner voices impeling them to commit suicide or acts of violence. Of course, we do not automatically accept that what a person tells us is accurate. The person may be under delusion, or may be unconsciously exaggerating symptoms to gain attention, or may simply be mistaken. However, we do take seriously what the afflicted person tells us and include it in our discernment.

o **Outward symptoms of demonic influence.** Occasionally during prayer for healing or while at Mass or listening to anointed preaching, a person begins to manifest signs of demonic influence. These may include bodily contortions, facial contortions, a marked change in the person's tone of voice (for instance, becoming harsh or guttural), or a sudden sneering or mocking attitude. Or we may notice an inexplicable unpleasant odor or a sudden cold in the room.

o **Bondage to a pattern of sin or negative behavior** (see Section 3.2.3). Another sign of demonic influence is an intractable pattern of sin—for instance, fits of rage, or compulsive lying, or the use of pornography—such that a person confesses it again and again but cannot get free. This is usually because by repeated acts of sin the person has given the evil one a foothold in his mind and will, so that his freedom is now compromised. Negative behaviors might include, for example, a persistent tendency to isolate oneself or a possessive relationship to a person.

o **An inner oppression** (see Section 3.2.3). A person may be oppressed by intense and persistent negative emotions or thought patterns—for instance, a sense of helplessness, hopelessness, rejection, abandonment, unworthiness, bitterness, guilt, fear, or anxiety, which keeps one from the fullness of life that is our inheritance as children of God (cf. Jn 10:10). Although such oppressive thoughts can be caused by emotional disorders, they may also be signs of demonic influence.

Although these criteria are useful, it is important to keep in mind that discernment can never be reduced to method or criteria alone. The ability to discern evil spirits often grows through long experience in deliverance ministry. In addition, some people have the charism that St. Paul calls "discernment of spirits" (1 Cor 12:10)—a supernatural, God-given ability to perceive what Spirit or spirits are operating in a given situation. People with this gift can sense whether someone is being influenced by the Holy Spirit, by merely human or natural causes, or by an evil spirit. Of course, a person's claim to have this gift is not a guarantee that they indeed have the gift. Like all gifts of the Spirit, the gift of discernment of spirits must be tested over time to prove its accuracy.

5.2.2 When Deliverance Ministry Is Not Appropriate

There are several circumstances in which it is not appropriate to do deliverance ministry.

o **In a case of possession.** A person is considered to be possessed if an evil spirit has gained control of not only aspects of his mind or emotions, but even his body, such that the demon can speak and act through the person. The Church's rite of exorcism lists certain signs indicating that a person may be possessed:

> According to approved practice, the following are regarded as signs of demonic possession: extended utterance in an unknown tongue, or the ability to understand such utterance; the power to reveal what is distant and hidden;

and the displaying of physical strength beyond what is appropriate to one's years, or natural state. These signs can offer some indication. But since signs of this sort are not necessarily to be considered of devilish provenance, attention should be paid to other factors, especially in the realm of the moral and spiritual, which can in a different way be evidence of diabolic intrusion. Examples of this are a violent aversion to God, the Most Holy Name of Jesus, the Blessed Virgin Mary and the Saints, the word of God, holy things, holy rites (especially of a sacramental nature) and holy images. And finally, careful consideration must be given to the manner in which all signs relate to faith and the spiritual struggle in the Christian life; for indeed, the Evil One is, above all, the enemy of God and of all that unites the faithful to the saving work of God.[3]

Exorcists all agree that cases of possession are very rare. In the vast majority of cases, demons have infested a certain area of a person's life but have not gained full control. We should therefore be extremely hesitant to conclude that a person is possessed. In a setting where there is deliverance ministry, a person may temporarily manifest signs of demonic control but without actually being possessed.

Where there is good reason to think a person is possessed, we must not attempt to do deliverance ministry, but instead refer the person to an authorized exorcist of the diocese. A person subject to such severe demonic bondage is in need of solemn exorcism through the authority Christ has entrusted to the Church. We should *not* tell the person he is possessed, but simply say we are referring him to an exorcist who will be able to do further discernment.

○ **In a case of mental disorder.** If the person shows symptoms of mental illness (for instance, if their speech is incoherent or they seem out of touch with reality), then they may be in need of professional help. This does not preclude our praying a simple prayer for deliverance, but we should avoid giving the person the impression that their problem is caused by demons or can be solved by deliverance.

○ **In a case where a person is seeking deliverance for someone else.** People sometimes come forward at conferences and seminars to ask for deliverance on behalf of a loved one. Intercessory prayer can indeed be a powerful means of grace for an afflicted person, just as in the Gospel accounts of a mother pleading for her demonized daughter and a father for his son (Mt 15:22-28; 17:14-18). However, a person cannot receive deliverance on behalf of another. The afflicted person needs to exercise her own free will to renounce those things that have given a foothold to evil spirits and to give the Lord access to her heart.

5.3 Deliverance and Healing

As discussed in Section 3.3, deliverance usually goes hand-in-hand with inner healing, since the evil one is able to operate in human lives primarily through entryways we have opened to him, which are in turn often related to wounds experienced early in life. In response to painful events, a person internalizes lies that ultimately come from the devil, the father of lies (Jn 8:44). Although each person's response to the difficulties in life is unique, based on his or her personality and circumstances, the devil's strategy is always the same: to deceive us by portraying God as not caring for us, just as he did in the garden (Gen 3:1, 4-5) and to undermine our identity as men and women created in the image of God (cf. Mt 4:3, 6).

Deliverance ministry, then, is truly effective when it addresses these wounds, bringing the Lord's light and healing into the inner rooms of the soul. Once a wound is healed, evil spirits are robbed of a point of access by which they were able to exert influence and hold a person captive. Once the Lord's light has come into an area where there was faulty thinking, evil spirits are deprived of their ability to deceive and manipulate a person in that area.

To address healing together with deliverance is to place the primary focus on the human person rather than the evil spirit. It also has the advantage of involving the individual to the maximum degree in his or her own deliverance. The afflicted person takes responsibility for ways he has given a foothold to the devil (cf. Eph 4:27), and is empowered to take up the authority he has in Christ to reject the evil one and resist his influence. At the same time he experiences Christ's love and mercy, healing the hidden wounds of the soul.

In some cases, as we are praying for inner healing the person may begin to manifest demonic influence in a way that interferes with our attempts to dialogue with her. The person may become sleepy, or may avoid eye contact, or may fall to the floor or become rigid, or may make intimidating, threatening or mocking remarks. These are all tactics by which demons desperately attempt to block the deliverance and avoid being cast out. In such cases, we may speak a simple command to bind the demon, so as to continue with the dialogue and the prayer for healing and deliverance. For instance, *I bind you in the name of Jesus Christ.* Or we may say to the person, *In the name of Jesus, wake up and look at me.*

5.4   The Essential Elements of Deliverance Ministry

The form that deliverance ministry takes largely depends on the context. Wherever possible, deliverance is best done in a quiet setting with ample time for preparation, conversation and prayer with the afflicted person. The elements listed below are most effective in such a setting. In other settings, however, such as a healing service or large conference, there is less time to spend with each individual, so the form may need to be simplified. Deliverance ministry should, however, include the following elements insofar as possible.

5.4.1 Prayer

Deliverance should begin and end with prayer. We pray that the Holy Spirit will be present and guide us, that he will protect us from all demonic attack, that he will bring to light whatever is necessary for the person's deliverance, that he will release them from all the evil that is oppressing them and that his love and mercy will overflow upon them. We can call on the angels and saints, especially St. Michael, to help and guard us.

5.4.2 Interview

Interviewing the person before doing deliverance is important for discerning the causes of the demonic oppression or bondage. In some cases there is opportunity for only one conversation, but deliverance is often most fruitful where there is more than one—for instance, during regular spiritual direction, or a retreat oriented to healing and deliverance, or an ordinary retreat.

The conversation should be relaxed and put the person at ease. At all times we must speak with delicacy, gentleness, and respect. Before asking questions, we should reassure the person that Jesus came to set the oppressed free. God has a wonderful plan for their life and delights in liberating them through the power of Jesus' cross and resurrection.

Questions like the following can be helpful:

What symptoms are you experiencing that have led you to seek deliverance or healing?

When did they begin?

Have you experienced any painful or traumatic events that may be linked to what you are experiencing? Or have you had hurtful relationships, especially in your family of origin? If so, have you forgiven the person or persons who offended you?

Have you ever participated in any occult activity, even in seemingly innocent fun?

Has there been any sin in your life that may also have contributed to this situation? If so, have you confessed it?

Where there is a serious unconfessed sin, if possible it is best for the person to go to the sacrament of Reconciliation before receiving deliverance ministry. In some cases, however, it is only after receiving deliverance ministry that the person is able to honestly acknowledge and express contrition for the sin. This needs to be discerned on a case-by-case basis.

5.4.3   Encounter with Jesus

Deliverance is always at the same time an encounter with Jesus. It should always be carried out in the context of evangelization, even for those who are already practicing Catholics. Everyone needs to hear again and again the saving message of the gospel: God so loved us that he sent his Son to die for us, to forgive our sins and bring us into eternal life. The deliverance minister should seek to be in the background, so to speak, and let the Lord be in the foreground. The goal is to bring the person into a personal relationship with Jesus, since only in him is there the fullness of freedom.

Before praying for deliverance, we should invite the afflicted person to make an explicit act of faith in Jesus, since deliverance from evil is his work, not ours. Victory over the evil one was won for us at the price of his suffering and death on the cross. Being liberated by Jesus begins with acknowledging that God's only Son became man and laid down his life *for me*, for my sins, for my salvation. Even those who have gone to church all their life may not have ever made this personal surrender to Jesus in faith. When they do so, it is a moment of conversion and the beginning of a lifelong journey of following Jesus as his disciple.

Even if the afflicted person is not a Christian, he or she should be invited to make a simple act of faith in Jesus. Very often the experience of being liberated from demonic bondage by Jesus is what puts a person on the path toward becoming a Christian. We should keep in mind, however, that an unbaptized person does not have the authority over demons in Christ that a baptized Christian has; he or she is thus more dependent on the deliverance minister.

As a general principle, if the afflicted person is not ready to put faith in Jesus in at least a tentative way, we should not pray with them for deliverance, since doing so risks giving the impression that deliverance is a kind of magic or occult activity involving anonymous spiritual powers. Instead we can pray a simple prayer of blessing and invite the person to come back for ministry if they do choose to believe in Jesus. There are, however, exceptions to this principle in large gatherings or where the afflicted person is not able to respond in faith until after they have received deliverance.

In some parts of the world, many non-Christians come to charismatic conferences and retreats to seek deliverance. Deliverance ministry must always be linked with evangelization and an invitation to conversion; the goal is to bring peo-

ple into the fullness of liberation, which comes in a relationship with Christ through faith and baptism.

5.4.4 Repentance

More than anything else, it is sin that opens a door to the
evil one. The kinds of sin most likely to lead to demonic
bondage are grave sins, such as murder; sins that have become habitual, such as hatred of another person; or sins of
forbidden spiritual activity, such as witchcraft. But as noted
above, even lesser sins can give the enemy a foothold by
which to deceive and oppress us. As long as a person has not
repented, the door remains open, and even if a demon seems
to be expelled, it may soon come back. To be freed from demonic influence, we must repent humbly and sincerely for
our sin. Once we have done so, we can be assured of God's
forgiveness. "If we confess our sins, he is faithful and just, and
will forgive our sins and cleanse us from all unrighteousness"
(1 Jn 1:9). The door is closed to the devil and instead becomes an open door for God's grace and mercy to flow into
one's life.

Sometimes a person needs the light of God to see and
honestly name their sins. Sins can be hidden in dark areas of
the heart, covered with layers of self-righteousness and self-
justification. A person may be blind, for instance, to their
deep-rooted jealousy, or unbelief, or self-pity, or judgment of
others. If it seems appropriate we can encourage the afflicted
person to pray with the psalmist,

Search me, O God, and know my heart!
Try me and know my thoughts! (Ps 139:23)

The Lord will faithfully answer this prayer, even though it often takes time to uncover hidden layers of sin.

If it becomes clear during ministry that a person remains attached to a serious sin (for instance, adultery), and is unwilling even to pray for the grace to be freed from it, then it is best to end the ministry session. We can explain that deliverance may have no lasting effect as long as one continues to invite the presence of the evil one through serious sin, and encourage the person to keep seeking God and to come back for ministry when they are ready to give up the sin.

5.4.5   Forgiveness of Others

One of the most important factors in being released from demonic bondage is forgiveness. As noted in Section 5.3, evil spirits can gain a foothold through the wounds left by traumatic events or hurtful relationships. To open ourselves to the Lord's work of liberation, we must be willing to forgive those who offended us. Forgiveness breaks the hold that that wound has on us and opens us to God's grace and healing.

Since there are many misconceptions about forgiveness, the deliverance minister may need to help a person understand what forgiveness is and is not.

o   To forgive is not to minimize a sin committed against us or "sweep it under the rug." It is not to exonerate the offender by saying that he probably meant well. Rather, forgiveness means acknowledging that I have been offended, but I choose to leave that offense in the hands of God. I choose to let go of my right to hold it against the other person, and instead let God be the judge.

o Forgiveness is not dependent on the offender repenting for his sin. It is very good if he does, but often an offender is unable or unwilling to repent, or in some cases is deceased. Although reconciliation requires the cooperation of both parties in a relationship, forgiveness can be practiced by one party alone.

o Some people are afraid of forgiving because they think it means returning to an unsafe situation, for instance, living with an abusive spouse. But the question of how to protect oneself in such a situation is distinct from the question of forgiveness. Forgiveness does not mean subjecting oneself to a situation of danger or abuse.

o Finally, forgiveness is an act of the will, which we make by the grace of God. We are able to forgive because we ourselves have been forgiven by God out of his abundant mercy (cf. Eph 4:32). We can choose to forgive even if our emotions still feel conflicted. That decision may need to be ratified repeatedly, but if we are sincere our emotions will eventually follow.

Sometimes a hurt is deeply buried. An offense that the person has not thought about in a long time may still be affecting their life. If it comes to mind during deliverance prayer, it may be because the Holy Spirit is revealing their need to forgive.

Where there is need for forgiveness, the deliverance minister should gently invite the person to speak words of forgiveness aloud, mentioning the offense if appropriate. For instance, *In the name of Jesus I forgive so-and-so for sexually abusing me. I forgive my father for never showing me affection. I forgive my wife for all the times she criticized me. I forgive the person who robbed my house twenty years ago.*

5.4.6 Renouncing the Works of Satan

Renunciation is related to repentance, but it is broader because it applies not only to sin but also to other effects of the evil one that have held us captive, such as fear, guilt, and shame. Becoming free from the oppression of Satan includes taking responsibility for ways we have accommodated or consented to these negative influences, and choosing to reject them in the authority of the name of Jesus. In the rite of baptism for adults the candidate is asked, "Do you renounce Satan... and all his works... and all his empty show?" It is an invitation to refuse, repudiate, and break any ties with the influence of the enemy—an invitation we embrace every time we renew our baptismal promises.

An important part of deliverance ministry is to lead the person in renouncing any spirits they recognize at work in their lives, especially those that come to light when recalling wounds from the past. This may include, for instance, negative patterns of thought, lies, an unholy tie to a person, or past involvement in the occult. Renunciation is effective when it is specific. For instance, *I renounce a spirit of shame in the name of Jesus. I renounce a spirit of abandonment in the name of Jesus.* The deliverance minister may also be led by the Holy Spirit to mention certain spirits that he senses may be at work. However, we should speak tentatively, respecting the afflicted person's freedom to confirm or not confirm what we think is going on.

5.4.7   The Word of Command

As noted in Section 3.5.3, direct commands to demons have an important role in deliverance. Through faith and baptism into Christ, demons are made subject to our authority (Lk 10:19).[4] This does not mean, however, that direct commands must be used on every occasion. In certain contexts they are not helpful; for instance, commanding demons may frighten the afflicted person if there is no time for an explanation. We must use common sense in discerning when to do so. In some circumstances it may be best to command demons silently; for instance, if a priest in the confessional senses that the penitent may need deliverance but he does not know if the person knows what deliverance is.[5] Although demons cannot read our minds, we should have no doubt: God will ensure that they hear those silent commands.

It is important to maintain a very basic distinction: we do not speak commands to God. We *pray* to God (which means plead or entreat), our Creator and Lord, with reverence and love. On the other hand, we do not plead with demons. The only appropriate way of speaking to them is by commands.[6] In traditional language, we adjure them, that is, command them in the name of God or Jesus (see Section 3.5.3).

The word of command should be very simple. For instance, "Spirit of lust, in the name of Jesus I command you to cease afflicting this person. Leave him and do not come back."

This is the way St. Paul spoke to the fortune-telling spirit that was afflicting a young girl: "I command you in the name of Jesus Christ to come out of her" (Acts 16:18). It is not necessary to tell the demon where to go, although it is acceptable to say something like "Go to the foot of the cross," or "Go to Jesus Christ." Of course one should never make use of superstitious practices like telling a demon to go to a holy person or to some earthly location.

The afflicted person himself may join in the command if he wishes. In fact, to do so helps him understand and take up the authority over evil spirits that he has in Christ.

There is no need to shout or bluster while commanding demons; in fact, doing so may only convince demons that we are insecure in our authority in Christ. It may also needlessly frighten the afflicted person, who might think we are shouting at them. Our primary focus must always be on the person. We must take care to treat them with unwavering compassion, respect and gentleness.

How do we know if the evil spirit or spirits have actually been cast out? Often the afflicted person will feel something lifting from them. They may have a sensation of relief or freedom. Often there is an evident change, as the person becomes peaceful and calm. In addition, if a team member has the charism of discernment of spirits, that gift will help in discerning whether any spirits remain.

What if it seems the evil spirits have not been cast out? Sometimes a person is in need of several sessions of deliverance over a period of weeks or months, especially if evil spirits have become deeply rooted in more than one area of their life. There may be layers of spiritual bondage. The person may need time to allow areas of woundedness to come to light, and to expose patterns of sin and bondage. We must also recall Jesus' words regarding certain demons: "This kind can only come out through prayer and fasting" (Mk 9:29), or through great faith (Mt 17:20). In such cases, we can reassure the person by emphasizing how courageous they are and how far they have already come by entering into a process of repenting, forgiving, and renouncing. We can affirm that the Father is pleased with them and has more for them. We can encourage them to keep seeking the Lord and to come and receive ministry again when they are ready.

5.4.8   Prayer for Infilling with the Holy Spirit

To cast out demons is only half the work of deliverance. The place formerly occupied by the enemy must now be filled with the Holy Spirit, who is the love of God poured into our hearts (cf. Rom 5:5). We should never end a deliverance session leaving this inner space empty. Instead, we invite the person to ask the Holy Spirit to come and fill the area of their life where they were previously bound and oppressed. We then pray for an outpouring of the Holy Spirit into their heart. We can pray specifically for the Spirit of truth to come and replace the lies and confusion in their heart with the truth of Jesus (cf. Jn 15:26); for the Spirit of peace to replace fear and anxiety; for the Spirit of joy to replace sadness and depression (Rom 14:17); for the Spirit of holiness to replace impurity (Rom 1:4); for the Spirit of love to replace hatred and bitterness (Rom 5:5).[7] It is especially important to speak blessing to the person, proclaiming the truth of their identity as a beloved son or daughter of God. The Holy Spirit acts as the truth is being verbally expressed, bringing confirmation.

Jesus teaches us to ask for the Holy Spirit with unbounded confidence: "for everyone who asks receives, and he who seeks finds, and to him who knocks it will be opened. What father among you, if his son asks for a fish, will instead of a fish give him a serpent; or if he asks for an egg, will give him a scorpion? If you then, who are evil, know how to give good gifts to your children, how much more will the heavenly Father give the Holy Spirit to those who ask him!" (Lk 11:10-13).

5.4.9 Concluding Advice

After concluding deliverance ministry, we should provide instruction on how the person can maintain their freedom from evil spirits by deepening her relationship with Christ through the Church. This includes the sacramental life, daily prayer and Scripture reading, putting off sin, growing in virtue, participating in some form of small group or community, and the use of sacramentals like holy water. It also entails establishing step-by-step the disciplines of a healthy lifestyle and fulfilling the normal duties of one's state of life.

Another neglected but powerful way of strengthening one's victory over evil spirits is to worship and glorify God. We can praise God in our own hearts throughout the day, in prayer meetings with others, and most of all in the celebration of the Eucharist. In the Eucharist we celebrate Christ's definitive victory over Satan, we fix our gaze on him, and we give him praise and thanks in the company of the faithful—

and all this in itself frees us from "from the snares of evil, from all the idolatries that lie in wait for us and enslave us."[8]

If during the time of ministry it came to light that the person has any unconfessed serious sin, or any pattern of sin that may be related to the demonic influence (for instance, bitterness, unforgiveness, jealousy, or lust), we encourage them to make use of the sacrament of Reconciliation as soon as possible.

If the person has been involved in the occult, we should instruct them to completely purge their home and their life of any unholy objects, including occult games, books, amulets, charms, statues, symbols, and so on. Instead they should place holy pictures, icons, or statues in their home to remind them of the Lord and lift their minds to heavenly realities.

5.4.10 Concluding Prayer

It is always good to end deliverance ministry with a prayer, rejoicing, thanking and blessing God for what he has done. We may also pray a cleansing prayer, asking the Lord to protect us from all harm and to free us from any negative spiritual influences we may have picked up during the ministry (especially if we are vulnerable in the same area as the person we have ministered to). It is best to avoid extremely long and complicated cleansing prayers, which can actually arouse fear and draw undue attention to demons. We must avoid an unhealthy fear of demonic reprisals against those doing deliverance ministry. As Origen, a third-century Church Father, exhorted,

Christians have nothing to fear, even if demons should not be well disposed to them; for they are protected by the supreme God, who is well pleased with their piety, and who sets his divine angels to watch over those who are worthy of such guardianship, so that they can suffer nothing from demons.... "The Lord is my light and my salvation; whom shall I fear? The Lord is the strength of my life; of whom shall I be afraid? Though an host should encamp against me, my heart shall not fear."[9]

St. Teresa of Avila likewise advises,

Not a fig shall I care then for all the devils in hell: it is they who will fear me. I do not understand these fears. "Oh, the devil, the devil!" we say, when we might be saying "God! God!" and making the devil tremble. Of course we might, for we know he cannot move a finger unless the Lord permits it. Whatever are we thinking of! I am quite sure I am more afraid of people who are themselves terrified of the devil than I am of the devil himself. For he cannot harm me in the least.[10]

And St. Thérèse of Lisieux, who at age four had a dream in which devils ran from her in terror, wrote,

A soul in the state of grace has nothing to fear from demons, who are cowards, capable of fleeing before the gaze of a little child![11]

5.5 Follow-Up to Deliverance

As noted in Section 3.1, deliverance is never an end in itself. *Freedom from* demonic influence is always for the sake of *freedom for* the fullness of life in relationship with God. The fullness of life comes in relationships of self-giving love with God and others, lived out in our particular vocation and in all the circumstances of life. As Vatican Council II teaches, "man, who is the only creature on earth which God willed for itself, cannot fully find himself except through a sincere gift of himself (cf. Lk 17:33)."[12] Liberation from demonic oppression empowers us to give and receive love with deeper authenticity and selflessness.

Insofar as possible, deliverance ministry should always be done in a setting that ensures opportunities for growth in the Christian life through individual and communal prayer, the reading of Scripture, the support of brothers and sisters, and the special graces offered by the sacraments. To do deliverance for an unconverted person and then simply send them on their way in a secular environment would do a great disservice—it would even be putting the person at risk of falling into deeper spiritual bondage (cf. Lk 11:24-26).

Once delivered, a person often remains fragile in the specific areas of bondage from which they were delivered. They will need to take steps to change long-established patterns of thought. A person who was bound by a spirit of pornography, for example, may need to move his computer into a public area, join a support group, establish a habit of daily prayer, and make a concrete plan for dealing with times of temptation.

In some cases, it becomes evident that the person receiving deliverance wants to have their problem solved but does not want salvation in Christ. They want a quick fix, so they can keep on living the life they were living before, apart from God. The deliverance minister should strive to correct this mentality insofar as possible, explaining that deliverance can never be lasting or complete without conversion to Christ and being filled with his Spirit. However, we can never coerce a person; there must always be a deep respect for free will. Jesus healed people even in cases where they had no apparent interest in a relationship with him (Lk 17:17-18; Jn 5:14-15). We can let go and prayerfully entrust the person to God, hoping that a time will come later on when they decide to surrender to Christ.

5.6 What Must Be Avoided in Deliverance Ministry?

Part of the reason that not all are called to deliverance ministry is because of the numerous pitfalls into which it is possible to fall. These errors can cause serious harm to the person receiving ministry, and even to the deliverance minister himself. This is not a reason to be frightened, but to be "sober and watchful; your adversary the devil prowls around like a roaring lion, seeking someone to devour" (1 Pet 5:8). The following list, while not exhaustive, explains some of the most important mistakes to avoid.

5.6.1   *Lack of Discernment*

o **Confusing natural causes with demonic influence.**
   Just as Eve attempted to cover for her sin by blaming
   the serpent (Gen 3:13), there can be a temptation on
   the part of an afflicted individual to too quickly blame
   their problems on the devil rather than taking personal responsibility. Likewise the deliverance minister can be tempted to do deliverance ministry without discerning what human factors are involved,
   whether they be sin, inner wounds, or emotional or
   psychological problems.

o **Getting in over our heads.** It would be foolish to attempt deliverance without discerning whether it is a
   case of more severe demonic oppression than we are
   equipped to handle. If we find that a situation is in
   fact beyond our ability, we can pray a simple prayer
   of blessing and refer the person to someone with
   more knowledge and experience. If we are not sure,
   we can lay hands on the person, pray in tongues, and
   ask the Holy Spirit for guidance. It is best to err on the
   side of caution. There are times, however, when God
   gives special grace for an "emergency" situation,
   when no one else is available to help the afflicted person.

5.6.2   *Deliverance for Personal Gain*

o **Self-promotion.** In any spiritual endeavor, there is
   always a danger of being motivated, even in subtle

ways, by a desire for importance, recognition, or human esteem. There can be a "need to be needed." Or there can be a desire for power. Jesus admonished his disciples not to exult in their authority over evil spirits, but in the fact that they belonged to him (Lk 10:20). For these reasons it is essential that those in deliverance ministry pray for the grace of humility and purity of heart, examine their conscience regularly, go to confession frequently, and hold themselves accountable to a good spiritual director or a Christian faith-sharing group.

o **Receiving payment for deliverance ministry.** Jesus instructed his disciples, "Heal the sick... cast out demons. You received without paying; give without pay" (Mt 10:8). Scripture pronounces very severe judgment on those who seek to buy or sell spiritual benefits that are in reality free gifts of God. Among those who succumbed to this temptation are Gehazi the servant of Elisha (2 Kg 5:20-27) and Simon the magician (Acts 8:18-23). On the other hand, there is nothing wrong with asking people for freewill donations, especially to support people who serve full-time in deliverance ministry. It is also reasonable to charge fees for conferences, workshops, books, and training materials. But payment should never be a condition for ministering to a person.

5.6.3 *Giving Ground to Demons*

o **Excessive focus on the demonic.** Demons have numerous tactics for turning our attention to an unhealthy focus on the demonic realm, which can be a distraction at best and spiritually dangerous at worst. We need to be vigilant against these tactics and ensure that our focus remains firmly fixed on God and on the person receiving ministry. It is important not to be motivated by curiosity or listen to descriptive details of evil that are not necessary to the process. The enemy wants to put into our imagination and memory images of evil that we should not entertain.

o **Dialogue with demons.** Church teaching contains clear warnings against any form of conversation with demons, including asking them questions, seeking information from them, or asking them for favors.[13] Our only interactions with demons should be simple commands to bind, silence, or expel them. If a demon taunts or threatens or otherwise seeks to engage our attention, we should ignore it and instead address the human person in front of us. There are exceptions in the case of authorized exorcists, who may question demons, but these exceptions do not apply to deliverance ministry.

o **Superstitious practices.** It goes without saying that there is no place for occult or superstitious practices in deliverance ministry. These would include, for example, using occult objects, telling a demon to go to a holy person or a particular object, or telling the afflicted person that he or she must carry out specific actions in order to be delivered. Although it is important to have a good grasp of proper practice, deliverance is not brought about by techniques or methods in themselves, but rather by the authority of Jesus Christ through our faith in him.

o **Sensationalism.** Deliverance ministry is not helped by stirring up drama, theatrics, or sensationalism, which only serve to draw undue attention to demons. When Jesus saw that a crowd was beginning to gather around an epileptic boy who had an evil spirit, he expelled the demon with a simple word of command (Mk 9:25), avoiding the possibility of a public spectacle at the expense of the afflicted boy.

5.6.4   Lack of Respect for the Person

o **Inappropriate probing.** Information about a person's past is often important for deliverance, but questions must be asked with discretion, gentleness and respect. Let the person decide how much they want to reveal. Never dig for unnecessary details; never pressure a person to reveal more than they are comfortable revealing.

o **Abuses of confidentiality.** The person receiving deliverance has opened up very vulnerable areas of his or her life. It is essential to hold this information in strictest confidence and not share with others what you learned in a deliverance session, except in such a general way that the person could never be identified. There are a few exceptions, however, such as (1) where the afflicted person may be in danger of harming himself or others, or (2) where there is a need to seek advice or training from an experienced deliverance ministry leader.

○ **Misuse of words of knowledge.** A "word of knowledge" (cf. 1 Cor 12:8), as used in the Catholic Charismatic Renewal today, refers to supernatural knowledge of particular facts, such as a healing that God is about to work (cf. Acts 14:9), or the underlying cause of a condition. Words of knowledge can play an important role in deliverance. But they are not infallible. They should always be given prudently and in a tentative way, asking the person for confirmation. For example, "I sense that there may be a spirit of shame involved. Does that sound right to you?" Avoid overreaching with detailed words of knowledge that can in no way be verified. In praying for deliverance from familial or intergenerational spiritual bondage (see Section 3.3.4), it is prudent to stay within the bounds of what can be reasonably confirmed by memory or family history. Generational influences "to the third and fourth generation" (Ex 20:5)—or, looking backward, to one's grandparents or great-grandparents— can usually be verified. To go further is to risk entering the realm of imagination; for example, "There was a Freemason in your family tree ten generations ago, and he put a Masonic curse on your family." Such unverifiable words can cause fear and anxiety, for if there is one such curse, who is to say what other unknown curses might be affecting one's life?

o **Degrading or humiliating practices.** There is no place in deliverance ministry for anger or annoyance, nor for any practices that degrade, humiliate, or embarrass a person. Do not encourage demonic manifestations, which demons often use to cause distraction and avoid being expelled. If there are manifestations, take the person aside into a private area as soon as possible. Look the person in the eye and seek to get their attention. Speak to them rather than to the demon. What is most important is that the person receiving deliverance experiences Christ's love and mercy through you.

5.6.5 Spiritual Traps

o **Inappropriate sexual behavior.** The evil one will constantly be seeking to exploit any weak points in the character of the deliverance minister. Even highly respected priest exorcists have had public downfalls because they unwisely did exorcisms one-on-one with women and succumbed to sexual temptation. Common sense tells us that deliverance ministry should never be done one-on-one with a person of the opposite sex (except for priests in the confessional and with appropriate safeguards). It is always best to do deliverance ministry in pairs, where one person takes the lead and the other is primarily interceding.

It is best if at least one of the pair is the same sex as the person receiving ministry.

o **Emotional involvement.** A common temptation is to become emotionally involved in the personal drama of the person receiving ministry. For example, one can pick up their emotion of anger toward a person who has behaved badly. In deliverance as in any other ministry, it is essential to keep the proper boundaries and not become emotionally involved. It is also important to remember that there are two sides to every story. The role of the deliverance minister is to help the person receive liberation and healing in Christ, not to take sides in their relationship difficulties with others.

o **Creating a relation of dependency.** Another danger is to subtly create an unhealthy relationship of dependency where a person feels the need to keep coming back for ministry again and again, never getting completely free. It is true that sometimes more than one deliverance session is needed, and sometimes months or years later the Lord may reveal to the person deeper areas of bondage for which further prayer is needed. But the aim of the deliverance minister is always to help the person enter into full freedom in Christ, so that they no longer need regular ministry. Guarding against dependency may at times mean saying "no" to requests for ministry.

5.6.6   Lack of Respect for the Church

o   **Teachings contrary to Catholic doctrine.** Jesus said, "You will know the truth, and the truth will make you free" (Jn 8:32). There is no such thing as freedom apart from truth. To deny, downplay, or muddle the teachings of the Church would be helpful to no one; on the contrary, it can cause grave harm. It is essential for deliverance ministers to know the Catholic faith well and to continually deepen their knowledge, especially by studying Scripture and the Catechism. They should always be ready to explain why God's word, as interpreted by the Church, is a gift that leads us to life and happiness.

o   **Theological innovation.** Some people involved in deliverance ministry claim knowledge of matters that go beyond what God has revealed, for instance, details about the angelic and demonic realms. It is wise not to enter into such speculations, nor to communicate them to the person receiving ministry. Keep what is said about demons simple, and turn the person's attention instead to Jesus.

o   **Lack of respect for Church authority.** Scripture counsels us, "Obey your leaders and submit to them; for they are keeping watch over your souls, as men who will have to give account. Let them do this joyfully, and not sadly, for that would be of no advantage to you" (Heb 13:17). Deliverance ministers should remain in close communion with those in ecclesial authority. Even if at times pastors do not fully understand deliverance ministry or put undue limits on it, we need to respect these limits while at the same time continuing to dialogue and explain why we believe this ministry is important. Lack of respect for Church authority removes spiritual protection and gives deliverance ministry a bad name. On the other hand, obedience to rightful authority in itself gives spiritual strength and protection.

6
Conclusion

I will put enmity between you and the woman,
and between your seed and her seed;
he shall crush your head,
and you shall crush his heel.

– Genesis 3:15

At the dawn of history when Satan ensnared our first parents, inaugurating the tragic history of human sin and bondage, God promised the ultimate victory of his Son. History would be marked by a perpetual struggle against evil, but there would come into the world the "seed of the woman" who would crush the head of the serpent, destroying evil at its very origins (Gen 3:15). As St. John Paul II noted, "Mary, Mother of the Incarnate Word, is placed at the very center of that enmity, that struggle which accompanies the history of humanity on earth and the history of salvation itself."[1] Mary appears again in the book of Revelation as the woman "clothed with the sun, with the moon under her feet, and on her head a crown of twelve stars," whose children conquer Satan "by the blood of the Lamb and by the word of their testimony" (Rev 12:1, 11, 17).

The Virgin Mary has played a dramatic role in the struggle against evil at various times; for instance, her appearance as Our Lady of Guadalupe in Mexico in 1531 led to one of the most fruitful harvests of evangelization in history and an end to centuries of bloody human sacrifice. As Christians today engage in the spiritual battle, seeking deliverance from evil spirits for ourselves and others, we can have unbounded confidence in her intercession. Through her maternal help we can stand courageously against the enemy, sharing in Christ's mission of bringing liberty to captives. May her prayers cause deliverance ministry to flourish in the Church today as a powerful instrument of evangelization, leading many people to experience the glorious freedom of the children of God.

Notes

I. Introduction

[1] Pope Francis, Homily, October 11, 2013.

[2] The term "deliverance ministry" is explained in the glossary in Section 1.3.

[3] A pioneer in deliverance ministry as well as exorcism was Fr. Rufus Pereira of India (1933-2012), a leader in the Catholic Charismatic Renewal and founder of the International Association for Deliverance.

[4] Cf. Vatican Council II, *Gaudium et Spes*, 4.

[5] See, for instance, *Catechism of the Catholic Church* (CCC) par. 391, 395, 2581-2582; Pope Paul VI, General Audience of November 15, 1972; Pope John Paul II, General Audience of August 13, 1986; Pope Francis, Homilies of March 24, 2013; April 11, 2014; Sept. 29, 2014.

[6] As Cardinal Walter Kasper has pointed out, "First of all, it is necessary to make a pastoral examination of conscience and ask ourselves in a self-critical way: why have so many Christians left our Church? We must not begin by asking ourselves what is wrong within the Pentecostals, but what are our own pastoral deficiencies. How can we react to this new challenge with a liturgical, catechetical, pastoral and spiritual renewal?" (Address at the opening of Pope Benedict XVI's meeting with the College of Cardinals on Ecumenical Dialogue, Nov. 23, 2007).

⁷ See Vatican II, *Lumen Gentium* 4 and 12; *Decree on the Apostolate of the Laity* (*Apostolicam Actuositatem*); Pope John Paul II, *On the Vocation and the Mission of the Lay Faithful* (*Christifideles Laici*).

⁸ For more information on the Catholic Charismatic Renewal, see the book *Baptism in the Holy Spirit* (Rome: ICCRS, 2012).

⁹ Pope Francis, Address to the Renewal in the Holy Spirit Movement, July 3, 2015.

¹⁰ Deliverance ministry arose in the wider charismatic movement especially among non-denominational charismatics, Anglicans, and Catholics. Deliverance ministry is thus an area where Catholics and other Christians have learned from one another, in accord with Pope Francis' exhortation: "How many important things unite us! If we really believe in the abundantly free working of the Holy Spirit, we can learn so much from one another! It is not just about being better informed about others, but rather about reaping what the Spirit has sown in them, which is also meant to be a gift for us" (*The Joy of the Gospel*, 246).

¹¹ This document does not attempt to develop a demonology, nor to demonstrate the existence of demons and their influence. It takes for granted the Church's teaching, based on Scripture and the Church Fathers, that Satan and demons exercise a real influence in human life (CCC 391, 2113, 2854).

¹² The term "ministry" does not here refer to an official ministry of the Church, but to various forms of service to the Lord and his people (cf. this usage in Pope Benedict XVI, *Verbum Domini*, 77; Pope John Paul II, *Christifideles Laici*, 20).

¹³ The term "imprecatory" is sometimes incorrectly used as the opposite of deprecative (or deprecatory). In fact, imprecatory formulas are those that curse or invoke evil upon the adversary, as in the imprecatory psalms, in which the psalmist curses his enemies. In the Rite of Exorcism of 1614 (the only official text used for exorcisms in the Latin Rite until 1999) some, but not all, of the addresses to demons are imprecatory.

[14] Exorcism had the wider meaning in Catholic tradition, but today is usually used in the stricter sense as synonymous with major exorcism.

[15] Some authors use "obsession" synonymously with "oppression," while others make a distinction between them. To avoid confusion, this book will simply speak of "oppression."

2. Biblical Foundations

[1] The word is used in this ordinary sense, for instance, in Num 22:22; 1 Sam 29:4; 2 Sam 19:23; 1 Kg 11:14, 23.

[2] *Diabolos* is the word normally used to translate *satan* in the Septuagint, the ancient Greek translation of the Old Testament.

[3] The same incident is recounted in an earlier text, 2 Samuel 24:1, where the Lord rather than Satan incites David.

[4] The repeated description of the evil spirit as "from the LORD" (1 Sam 16:14-16, 23; 18:10; 19:9) must be read in light of the canon of Scripture as God's *permitting* the evil spirit to afflict Saul, with the ultimate aim of leading him to repentance (cf. 1 Cor 5:5; 2 Cor 12:7).

[5] There are some passages in which it is not clear whether an actual spiritual being is meant, or simply a human disposition (e.g., Num 5:14; Isa 19:14).

[6] Cf. CCC 407.

[7] "Exorcism" is the term commonly used for the casting out of demons by Jesus and the apostles. However, it should be noted that their activity differs from exorcism in the modern sense in that it did not involve a liturgical rite, but simply a word of command. Moreover, it included both exorcism of the possessed and deliverance of those suffering lesser forms of demonic affliction.

[8] The New Testament word translated "possessed with demons" is *daimonizomenos* (literally, "demonized"), a term that probably applies to a broad range of forms of demonic affliction.

[9] Cf. the exorcism recounted by Josephus, *Jewish Antiquities*, 8.2.5, in which the exorcist uses an odiferous root and adjures the demon in the name of Solomon.

[10] Cf. CCC 547-550.

[11] The Greek word for "liberty" (*aphesis*), used twice in Luke 4:18, is the same word often used for "forgiveness" of sins (Lk 1:77; 3:3; 24:47).

[12] The evangelists' description of the man evokes Isaiah 65:4, which describes sinful Israel as "living among the tombs and... eating swine's flesh."

[13] The earliest manuscripts of the Gospel lack the phrase "and fasting."

[14] A less clear example is in Mark 1:43, where Jesus' admonition to the healed leper ("he sternly charged him and sent him away") could be translated "he rebuked it and cast it out," implying that Jesus delivered the man from a spirit of leprosy.

[15] Some ancient manuscripts read seventy-two. The discrepancy is probably due to the allusion to Num 11:25-30, where seventy elders, including two who remained in the camp, receive a share of Moses' spirit.

[16] Literally, "a python spirit." In Greek mythology, the python was a serpent killed by the god Apollo. Greek pagans considered the python to be the guardian of the oracle at Delphi, a shrine associated with divination and fortune-telling.

[17] The Greek term for "opportunity" is literally "place" (*topos*); some translations render it "foothold."

3. Theological Context

[1] See the Congregation for the Doctrine of the Faith, "Christian Faith and Demonology" (1975), 1.

[2] Vatican Council II, *Sacrosanctum Concilium*, 6.

[3] Cardinal Léon-Joseph Suenens, *Renewal and the Powers of Darkness*, Malines Document 4 (Ann Arbor: Servant / London: Darton, Longman & Todd, 1983), 125.

[4] Vatican Council II, *Lumen Gentium* 3; see also Council of Trent (1562): DS 1740.

[5] Pope Paul VI, *Evangelii Nuntiandi*, 14.

[6] Pope Francis, *The Joy of the Gospel* (*Evangelii Gaudium*), 36.

7 St. John Cassian, *Conferences*, VII.24-25.

8 St. John Climacus, *The Ladder of Divine Ascent*, Step 15.74.

9 Ibid., 74-75.

10 See, for instance, Aquinas, *Summa Theologiae* I.114; *De Malo*, 16.8, 11-12.

11 See Ignatius of Loyola, *Spiritual Exercises*, no. 314-315. Ignatius speaks of "the evil spirit" or "the enemy" in a broad sense, referring both to demons and to the tendencies in our own psyches that arise from pride and disordered desires. He likewise uses "the good spirit" to refer both to God and to all the influences for good that surround us, including the angels and saints.

12 See, e.g., St. Francis of Sales, *Introduction to the Devout Life*, Part IV. For a synthesis of the teaching of Carmelite saints on the action of demons, see Marie-Eugène de l'Enfant-Jésus, *Je veux voir Dieu* (Editions du Carmel, 2014), VII.

13 See Thomas Aquinas, *De Veritate*, q. 22 a.5.

14 See CCC 405.

15 See Thomas Aquinas, *Summa Theologica* I-II, q. 80.

16 "The devil exercises over sinners only a moral influence, which is moreover measured to the welcome which the individual gives to his inspiration (Jn 8:38, 44). If people carry out his desires (Jn 8:44) and do 'his work' (Jn 8:41), they do so freely" (Congregation for the Doctrine of the Faith, "Christian Faith and Demonology," 4).

17 For a more detailed scale see Francis MacNutt, *Deliverance from Evil Spirits: A Practical Manual* (Grand Rapids: Chosen, 2009), 207-211.

18 See CCC 1673; Code of Canon Law 1172.

19 Aquinas underlines how a promise "perfects", "strengthens", "solidifies" or "stabilizes" our will (see *Summa Theologica* II-II, q. 88).

20 See for example Thomas Aquinas, *Summa Theologica* I-II, q. 80 a. 2 resp.

[21] Self-inflicted curses fall into the category of occult practices that entail a personal involvement and do not need any particular explanation.

[22] See MacNutt, *Deliverance from Evil Spirits*, 102-104.

[23] "Adam is the principle of present life for all men, in such a way that we all form a unique person through our common nature, since each of us is a member of the same species" (Theodore of Mopsuestia, *In Galatians* 3.28); see also Thomas Aquinas, *Summa Theologica* III, q. 8; Vatican Council II, *Gaudium et Spes*, 25; 32.

[24] Philosophers speak of "performative utterances," that is, statements that bring about what they say, such as: "I crown you as king"; "You are hired"; or in a wedding, "I do." The power of speech is also emphasized by the Scriptures: "No human being can tame the tongue. It is restless evil, full of deadly poison. With it we bless our Lord and Father, and with it we curse people who are made in the likeness of God. From the same mouth come blessing and cursing. My brethren, this ought not to be so" (Jas 3:8-10; cf. Gen 27; Num 6:23-27; Num 24).

[25] *Adjurare* is the Latin translation of the Greek *exorkizō*, from which the modern term "exorcise" is derived.

[26] Alphonsus Liguori (1696-1787), *Theologia Moralis*, Appendix de Adjuratione, §193.1 (Paris, 1835), 56.

[27] Aquinas, *Summa Theologica* II-II, q. 90, a. 2; see Alphonsus Liguori, *Theologia Moralis*, §193.4. Dominic Prümmer, *Manuale Theologiae Moralis*, 10th ed. (Barcelona: Editorial Herder, 1945), §463.

[28] Exorcism is, however, considered a sacramental (CCC 1673). Other sacramentals include, for example, blessings, the sign of the cross, holy water, blessed salt, blessed oil, crucifixes, and icons.

[29] In traditional theological language, sacraments are effective *ex opere operato* (simply by being celebrated) and sacramentals are effective *ex opere operantis Ecclesiae* (from the work and prayers of the Church).

4. Exorcism and Deliverance in Church History

[1] Ramsay MacMullen, *Christianizing the Roman Empire A.D. 100-400* (New Haven, Connecticut: Yale University Press, 1984), 27-28.

[2] Justin Martyr, *Second Apology*, 6.5-6; cf. *Dialogue with Trypho*, 30.3; 76.6; 85.2.

[3] Irenaeus, *Against Heresies*, 2.32.4.

[4] Tertullian, *The Shows*, 29.

[5] Origen, *Against Celsus*, 7.4; translation adapted from ANF, vol. 4. See also Tertullian, *Apologeticus*, 23.4.

[6] Cyprian, *Treatise to Donatus on the Grace of God*, paraphrased by Anne Field in *From Darkness to Light. What It Meant to Become a Christian in the Early Church* (Ann Arbor: Servant, 1978), 190-91.

[7] Hilary, *Tract on the Psalms* 64.14-15 (CSEL 22.246).

[8] See Francis Omara, *Exorcism in Church Law: Charism, Ministry and Canonical Regulation* (Pontifical Gregorian University dissertation, Rome, 2008), 26-27; 29-32.

[9] See Pope Cornelius (251-253 AD), quoted by Eusebius, *Church History* 6.43 (PG 20.622).

[10] The earliest mention of the ordination of exorcists is from the Fourth Council of Carthage (398 AD), canon 7; see Jeffrey Grob, *A Major Revision of the Discipline on Exorcism: A Comparative Study on the Liturgical Laws in the 1614 and 1998 Rites of Exorcism* (University of Ottawa, 2007), 51.

[11] The fourth-century document *Apostolic Constitutions*, 8.26, for instance, explicitly states that an exorcist is not ordained, "For he who has received the gift of healing is declared by revelation from God, the grace which is in him being manifest to all."

[12] See Omara, *Exorcism in Church Law*, 36-37; 45; *Rituale Romanum* (1614); Baruffaldo Ferrariensi, *Ad Rituale Romanum Commentaria* (Venice: Typographia Balleoniana, 1731), 358–359.

[13] See Omara, *Exorcism in Church Law*, 29.

[14] Canons 1151-1153; see Grob, *Major Revision*, 109.

[15] See Omara, *Exorcism in Church Law*, 36; 44 and 30; 47.

[16] Alphonsus Liguori, *Theologia Moralis*, §193.4; see also Dominic Prümmer, *Manuale Theologiae Moralis*, 10th ed. (Barcelona: Editorial Herder, 1945), §463.

[17] Hieronymus Noldin, *Summa Theologiae Moralis*, vol. III, *De Sacramentis* (Innsbruck, 1955[23]), 43.

[18] See, for example, Francisco Suárez (1548-1617), *De Adjuratione*, 4.11, in *Opera Omnia*, vol. XIV (L. Vivès, Paris, 1859), 742; St. Alphonsus Liguori, *Theologia Moralis*, §193.4.

[19] We are mainly following Ernest Caparros, Michel Thériault, Jean Thorn (eds.), *Code of Canon Law Annotated*, (Montréal: Wilson & Lafleur, 1993), 736.

[20] See Sacra Congregatio de Propaganda Fide, "Exorcismus in Satanam et angelos apostaticos," *Acta Sanctae Sedis* 23 (1890-1891), 743-747. Already from the 1952 edition of the *Rituale Romanum* this prayer is reserved to priests authorized by their Ordinaries and bishops (see Omara, *Exorcism in Church Law*, 53). It is important to note that this prayer is not the Prayer to St. Michael the Archangel, which all Catholics are encouraged to pray.

[21] *Interpellare* has a varied range of signification: it can mean to interrupt or break in on someone who is speaking with an objection; to disturb, obstruct or hinder someone; to summon; to press someone into doing something; and more rarely, just to address someone. The official translations of the CDF document in modern languages have chosen more precise terms that mean to question and/or to invoke to ask for information or for help: "to question" (English), "interrogare" (Italian), "befragen" (German), "interpeller" (French), "interpelar" (Spanish and Portuguese), "wzywac" (Polish). Only the French and the Portuguese have a wider meaning: the French means to address in a confrontational way, either to question or to insult, while the Portuguese covers most of the meanings of the Latin, though its first meaning is to question someone. These different translations, especially applied in the context of relating to

the spiritual world, clearly indicate that what is mainly at stake is to question or invoke a demon to obtain information or help.

5. Pastoral Guidelines

[1] The material in this chapter is drawn in part from Neal Lozano, *Unbound: A Practical Guide to Deliverance* (Grand Rapids, Mich.: Chosen, 2010); Francis MacNutt, *Deliverance from Evil Spirits: A Practical Manual* (Grand Rapids: Chosen, 2009); and Michael Scanlan and Randall Cirner, *Deliverance from Evil Spirits. A Weapon for Spiritual Warfare* (Cincinnati: Servant, 1980).

[2] Cf. Irenaeus, *Against Heresies* 2.32.4; Francisco Suárez, *De Adjuratione*, 4.11, in *Opera Omnia*, vol. XIV (L. Vivès, Paris, 1859), 742.

[3] *De exorcismis et supplicationibus quibusdam* (editio typica 1999), praenotanda, sec. 16, translated by Pierre Bellemare.

[4] Cf. St. Hilary, *Tract on the Psalms*, 64.15.

[5] Catholic moral theology has traditionally advised the use of the silent command in such cases. The silent command is prudent where the afflicted person is not prepared to receive or understand deliverance. Moreover, discernment of the need for a deliverance is not infallible. For instance, the penitent may primarily need to embark on a path of long-term growth in virtue and self-understanding.

[6] Aquinas, *Summa Theologica* II-II, q. 90, a. 2. As noted above, however, authorized exorcists may also question demons.

[7] See Francis MacNutt, *Deliverance from Evil Spirits*, 180.

[8] Suenens, *Renewal and the Powers of Darkness*, 188.

[9] Origen, *Against Celsus* 8.27.

[10] Teresa of Avila, *Autobiography*, ch. 25.

[11] Thérèse of Lisieux, *Story of a Soul*, ch. 1.

[12] *Gaudium et Spes*, 24.

[13] Congregation for the Doctrine of the Faith, *Inde ab aliquot*, 3 (see Section 4.4 above); cf. Thomas Aquinas, *Summa Theologica* II-II, q. 90, a. 2.

6. Conclusion

¹ Pope John Paul II, *Mother of the Redeemer* (*Redemptoris Mater*), 11.